Working with Words

CAMBRIDGE HANDBOOKS FOR LANGUAGE TEACHERS
General Editors: Michael Swan and Roger Bowers

This is a series of practical guides for teachers of English and other
languages. Illustrative examples are usually drawn from the field of English
as a foreign or second language, but the ideas and techniques described can
equally well be used in the teaching of any language.

In this series:

Drama Techniques in Language Learning – A resource book of
communication activities for language teachers
by Alan Maley and Alan Duff

Games for Language Learning
by Andrew Wright, David Betteridge and Michael Buckby

Discussions that Work – Task centred fluency practice *by Penny Ur*

Once Upon a Time – Using stories in the language classroom
by John Morgan and Mario Rinvolucri

Teaching Listening Comprehension *by Penny Ur*

Keep Talking – Communicative fluency activities for language teaching
by Friederike Klippel

Working with Words – A guide to teaching and learning vocabulary
by Ruth Gairns and Stuart Redman

Learner English – A teacher's guide to interference and other problems
edited by Michael Swan and Bernard Smith

Working with Words

A guide to teaching and learning vocabulary

Ruth Gairns and Stuart Redman

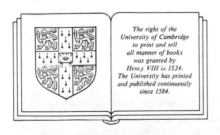

The right of the
University of Cambridge
to print and sell
all manner of books
was granted by
Henry VIII in 1534.
The University has printed
and published continuously
since 1584.

Cambridge University Press
Cambridge
London   New York   New Rochelle
Melbourne   Sydney

Published by the Press Syndicate of the University of Cambridge
The Pitt Building, Trumpington Street, Cambridge CB2 1RP
32 East 57th Street, New York, NY 10022, USA
10 Stamford Road, Oakleigh, Melbourne 3166, Australia

© Cambridge University Press 1986

First published 1986
Reprinted 1986

Printed in Great Britain at The Bath Press, Avon

Library of Congress catalogue card number: 85–30871

British Library cataloguing in publication data

Gairns, Ruth

Working with words: a guide to teaching and
learning vocabulary. – (Cambridge handbooks for
language teachers)
1. English language – Study and teaching –
Foreign speakers   2. Vocabulary – Study and
teaching
I. Title   II. Redman, Stuart
428.1   PE1128.A2

ISBN 0 521 26889 3 hard covers
ISBN 0 521 31709 6 paperback

BS

Contents

Contents

PART D VOCABULARY IN COURSE BOOKS

Acknowledgements

We are grateful to all the people who have helped us with this book. Our thanks to:

Our editor, Michael Swan, whose expert help and guidance has been invaluable to us throughout the writing of the book.

Mary Carline, and the other authors acknowledged throughout the book, for specific ideas we have borrowed.

Tim Lowe, Eddie Williams, and Jean Stokes, for guidance in shaping the book.

The teachers at International House (London), and The London School for English, for piloting the student activities and providing us with essential feedback on the material.

Paul Meara for his comments on the final manuscript.

And finally, to Margherita Baker, Peter Ducker and the Editorial Staff at CUP for all their efforts in making this book possible.

The authors and publishers are grateful to the following for permission to reproduce copyright material:
pp.4–5 and 128–9 extracts from the *Oxford Advanced Learner's Dictionary of Current English* edited by A. S. Hornby, pp.46 and 98 extracts from *Use your Dictionary* by Adrian Underhill, pp.180–1 extracts from *Streamline English: Connections* by Bernard Hartley and Peter Viney, reprinted by permission of Oxford University Press; p.11 article from the *Sunday Mirror* and pp.85, 116–7, 118 articles from the *Daily Mirror*, Syndication International Ltd; p.12 transcript of radio advertisement for Concorde Wine, Vine Products Group; pp.23–4 adapted text from *Themes* by Alan Matthews and Carol Read, Collins Educational; pp.28 and 29 extracts from the *Longman Active Study Dictionary*, pp.42 and 61 extracts from the *Longman Dictionary of Contempory English*, p.43 extracts from the *Longman Lexicon of Contempory English* edited by Tom McArthur, p.152 extract from *Storylines* by Mark Fletcher and David Burt, pp.174–5 extracts from *Studying Strategies* by Brian Abbs/Ingrid Freebairn with John Clegg/Norman Whitney, Longman Group Ltd; pp.38 and 41 extracts from *The Words you Need* by B. Rudska, J. Channel, Y. Putseys, P. Ostyn, Macmillan, London and Basingstoke; p.56 article reproduced by courtesy of *The Observer* London*; p.113 extract from *Play Games with English*: Book 1 by Colin Granger, illustrated by John Plumb, Heinemann Educational Books; pp.118 and 120 articles from *The Standard*, Express Newspapers p.l.c.; pp.121–2 by Peter Wilby from *The Sunday Times*, Times Newspapers Ltd; p. 170 extract from *Gyles Brandreth's Book of Puzzles and Brainteasers*, Octopus Books Ltd.

The Observer publishes a resource pack of authentic source material for teachers of EFL. In nine monthly packs, from October to June, over 150 *Observer* articles are used, each with a specially written worksheet and exercises. Available by subscription only, further details from: The Observer EFL Service, 8 St. Andrew's Hill, London EC4V 5JA.

Preface

In recent years, vocabulary has not received the recognition it deserves in the classroom. Not that it has been characterised by any neglect in terms of quantity. A vast amount of teaching time is consumed by explanation and definition, classroom blackboards are often littered with masses of new lexical items, and students compile page upon page of vocabulary word-lists that they rarely have the opportunity to practise. The simple fact is that vocabulary seems to arise in the classroom regardless of the chosen activity, and in spite of any conscious design on the teacher's part. Perhaps this is the root of the problem. Why should we go out of our way to select lexical items and invent classroom activities when there is a form of natural selection inherent in any classroom activity and an element of vocabulary teaching in every piece of classroom material? The answer lies in our assessment of what is useful and appropriate from this input. Can we assume that vocabulary arising incidentally in classroom materials will automatically be the most useful and appropriate to our students?

At this point it is relevant to consider the factors which distinguish 'street learning' from school learning. It is probably safe to assume that learners in an English-speaking country (and without the aid of formal instruction) will eventually uncover the vocabulary relevant to their individual needs. In a school learning situation with limited time available, conflicting student interests, and the constraints imposed by other syllabus demands, we cannot leave lexis to take care of itself in this random fashion and assume that students will acquire the vocabulary which best suits their needs.

In organising school learning, we have to select vocabulary carefully to ensure that high priority items are included, and provide varied opportunities for practice to compensate for the lack of repeated exposure available to the 'street learner'. It is the aim of this book to assist the teacher in making the most prudent selection and organisation of lexis for the classroom, and to offer as wide a range of practice ideas as we can summon up, in order to facilitate the kind of interesting generative practice without which effective learning cannot take place.

On the assumption that most people learn by doing, we have included a wide range of reader activities throughout the book. On the further assumption that people enjoy and benefit from feedback on their efforts,

1

we have included a key of suggested answers at the back of the book. We must stress, however, that the answers are not exhaustive (this would have required a second book), and some of the activities are far too subjective to offer more than a very personal and possibly biased opinion about the best answer. The *Further reader activities* in parts C and D do not have answers in the key.

Note: For convenience we have referred to the teacher and student throughout in the masculine form. This is not because we are assuming an all-male readership and all-male classes, but because of the inadequacies of the English pronoun system.

1   Language awareness activities

The activities which follow are intended as a practical introduction to some of the issues which are explored in chapters 2 and 3. They focus on typical problems learners encounter when acquiring vocabulary as well as on certain pedagogic questions.

You will find suggested answers in the key at the back of the book.

1   *READER ACTIVITY*

The utterances below were all made by foreign learners. The nationality of the speaker is given beside each example. Read each example and then answer the comprehension questions below each one. Afterwards, check your answer with the key at the back.

1 I've studied in a public school. (Italian)
   Q: Did the student pay, get a scholarship or have a free education?
2 I live in Sao Paolo which is a great city. (Brazilian)
   Q: Is the speaker giving factual information about Sao Paolo or expressing his opinion?
3 Can you tell me the way to the subway? (a Mexican at Piccadilly Circus)
   Q: Does the speaker want to cross the street or take a train?
4 I feel sorry for people who live in the suburbs. (Spanish)
   Q: Does the speaker think the suburbs are boring and middle-class, or ugly and poverty-stricken?
5 I'm not sure if that's possible – I'll have to look at my agenda. (French)
   Q: Is he going to look at the notes for a meeting or his diary?
6 The ski station is very pretty. (Tunisian)
   Q: Is the speaker talking about a railway station?

2   *READER ACTIVITY*

The three lists of words below are written in French, German and Spanish. Choose one of the languages with which you are not familiar and give what you feel to be an equivalent translation for each item.

French	*German*	*Spanish*
terrible	aktuell	contenta
librairie	singen	embarazada
furieux	famos	tímido
préparer	Menü	constipado
canne à pêche	kommen	movimiento

3 *READER ACTIVITY*

Look at the three items of vocabulary below. If you were going to teach
them to a general English class, which meaning and which grammatical
value would you teach first for each one? (The items are not related.)

picket   grant   record

Now look at the definitions of these items from the *Oxford Advanced
Learners Dictionary of Current English (OALDCE)*. The dictionary states that
definitions are listed in order of meaning from the most common or simple
to the most rare or complicated. Do you agree with their order?

pick·et /'pɪkɪt/ *n* **1** pointed stake, etc set upright in
the ground (as part of a fence, or to tether a horse
to). **2** small group of men on police duty, or sent
out to watch the enemy. **3** worker, or group of
workers, stationed at the gates of a factory, dock-
yard, etc during a strike, to try to persuade others
not to go to work: *a '∼ line,* line of ∼s, eg outside
a factory. **flying ∼,** ∼ formed of workers who do
not work at the place where the ∼ is stationed. □
vt, vi [VP6A,2A] **1** put ∼s(1) round; tether (a horse)
to a ∼(1). **2** place ∼s(2) in or round; station (men)
as ∼s. **3** place ∼s(3) at: *∼ a factory;* act as a
∼(3).

grant /grɑːnt *US:* grænt/ *vt* **1** [VP6A,12A,13A] con-
sent to give or allow (what is asked for): *∼ a
favour/request; ∼ sb permission/a request to do
sth. He was ∼ed a pension.* **2** [VP6A,9,25] agree
(that sth is true): *∼ the truth of what someone says;
∼ing this to be true/that this is true. I ∼ his
honesty/∼ that he is honest. He's an honest man, I
∼ you.* ***take sth for ∼ed,*** regard it as true or as
certain to happen. ***take sb for ∼ed,*** treat his
presence and actions as a due rather than a favour.
□ *n* sth ∼ed, eg money or land from a government:
*∼s towards the cost of a university education; ∼-
aided schools/students.*

rec·ord[1] /'rekɔːd *US:* 'rekərd/ *n* **1** [C] written account of facts, events, etc: *a ∼ of school
attendances/of road accidents; the (,Public) 'R∼
Office,* one in London where public documents
with accounts of events, official acts, etc written
down at the time they occur, are stored. **2** [U] state
of being ∼ed or preserved in writing, esp as
authentic evidence of sth: *a matter of ∼,* sth that is
established as fact by being ∼ed. ***be/go/put sb
on ∼:*** *It is on ∼ that the summer was the wettest
for 50 years. I don't want to go on ∼/don't want
you to put me on ∼ as saying that I think the Prime
Minister a fool.* ***off the ∼,*** (colloq) not for publication or for recording: *What the President said at
his press conference was off the ∼,* not to be
repeated by the newspaper men there, and not to be

used in their reports or articles. **3** [C] facts known about the past of sb or sth: *He has an honourable ~ of service/a good ~. Your ~ is in your favour,* What we know about your past is favourable to you. *That airline has a bad ~,* eg has had many accidents to its aircraft. **4** [C] sth that provides evidence or information: *Our museums are full of ~s of past history. R~s of ancient civilizations are still being excavated.* **5** [C] disc on which sound has been registered; what is ~ed on such a disc: *'gramophone ~s.* ⇨ recording. '**~-player** *n* instrument for reproducing sound from discs (often one connected to an external loud-speaker). **6** [C] limit, score, point, attainment, mark, etc (high or low), not reached before; (esp in sport) the best yet done: *Which country holds the ~ for the marathon? Two ~s fell during the sports meeting at Oslo last week.* (attrib) *Hill made a ~ score in the match against Kent,* (cricket) scored a total that was a ~. *There was a ~ rice crop in Thailand that year.* **break/beat the ~,** do better than has been done before. Hence, '**~-breaking** *adj*

re‧cord[2] /rɪˈkɔːd/ *vt* [VP6A] **1** set down in writing for reference; preserve for use, by writing or in other ways, eg on a disc, magnetic tape, videotape, film, etc: *This volume ~s the history of the regiment. The programme was ~ed.* Cf a *'live'* broadcast. *The tape-recorder has ~ed his voice and the camera has ~ed his features.* **~ing angel,** angel who, it is said, ~s men's good and bad actions. **2** (of an instrument) mark or indicate on a scale: *The thermometer ~ed 40°C.*

---

4 <u>*READER ACTIVITY*</u>   ⌐━─╣

Look at the way students have expressed themselves in the sentences below. In each case, can you suggest an idiomatic expression it would be appropriate for the student to learn?

e.g. 'When he told me women are not allowed on the underground, I knew he was *having a joke with me.*'

Answer: to pull someone's leg.

1 'In England, it is very bad to *go in front of someone else in* the queue.'
2 'Can you *take me in your car* to the station, John?'
3 'I was so tired when I went to bed last night that I *slept* immediately.'
4 'You are wearing your jumper *the wrong way*; I can see the label.'
5 'I had a terrible accident and my car was *completely damaged.*'
6 'Parents sometimes get angry because their children *do not thank them for their work.*'
7 'I can only study in England for one month so it is important for me *to take advantage of the time.*'
8 'I know a little hotel. It's *an unusual place and not many people go there,* but it's very nice.'

5

5 *READER ACTIVITY*

The sentences below are all typical learner utterances. What important feature of teaching do they highlight?

1 He made a complain about the food.
2 He's an economy lecturer.
3 I think the company needs to product more next year.
4 We devaluated our currency last year.
5 Kissinger is a politic.
6 It's a very analystical book.
7 My mother is a very good cooker.
8 You are very unpolite.

6 *READER ACTIVITY*

Look at the letter below. It contains several different errors, but which would you identify as being the area which requires the most *urgent* attention?

> Calle Uria, 24
> Madrid
> May 24th
>
> Dear Sir,
>
> I am a student of English in Spain and my teacher advised me that I write to you for informations.
>
> I want to make a course at London during the summer for one month and I would like that the course includes some Business English. I would prefer study on a course very intensive.
>
> Could you also suggest me where I can find accommodation in London?
>
> I look forward to hearing from you with all the informations.
>
> Yours sincerely,
>
> *Conchita Piquer.*
>
> Conchita Piquer.

7 READER ACTIVITY

Look at the groups of verbs below. Each group has a specific problem for students: in each case, there would be one in particular which would need pointing out to students. What is it in each different group? (You should have four different problems at the end of the exercise.)

Group 1
to bring   to take   to eat   to swim   to fall

Group 2
to rely   to depend   to insist   to apply

Group 3
to see   to hear   to want   to know   to smell

Group 4
to prefer   to enjoy   to dislike   to avoid

8 READER ACTIVITY

Students are often required to transform a whole passage into the plural form. Look at the passage below and make the necessary changes in the forms of nouns, verbs and pronouns. What areas can you identify as being a source of difficulty for learners? You should find five different types of potential error.

> The old woman, weighed down by heavy luggage, walked slowly along the corridor until she reached the check-in desk. The man in front of her was asking for information about the overdue flight while his wife was trying to control their hysterical child. A person near her was asking a policeman for advice about parking restrictions. The woman's patience was wearing thin.

9 READER ACTIVITY

What's the opposite of . . .
 dry?
 strong?
 rough?
 thick?
 hard?

Now give the opposite of the following:
 dry wine
 strong cigarettes
 a rough sea
 a thick person
 a hard exercise

What does this indicate about the very common practice of teaching 'opposites'?

10 *READER ACTIVITY*

In the groups below, cross out the 'wrong' answer in each case. What type of error is being made, and how can it be accounted for?

1
He made
| an arrangement.
| the bed.
| a photo.

2
He got off
| the plane.
| the taxi.
| his bike.

3
He lost
| his wallet so he went to the police.
| the bus so he was late.
| his way so he got very upset.

4
He did
| nothing all afternoon.
| his homework.
| an investment.

5 A fire
The lesson | broke out.
A war

11 *READER ACTIVITY*

The groups of multi-word verbs below represent different ways that one might approach the teaching of such verbs. What is the logic behind each approach and do you consider any of the approaches to be more suitable than others?

1 to put something on
to put somebody up
to put somebody/something off

2 to take something up
to look something up
to bring something up

3 to ring somebody up
to get through
to hang up

4
to take off
| clothes
| a person
| £5 (i.e. reduce)

12 *READER ACTIVITY*

In the sentences below, can you think of incorrect words that students might use in place of the italicised items? How would you account for these mistakes?

1 When I was younger, I used to enjoy sitting in the back *row* at the cinema.
2 We have a ten-minute *break* between each lesson.
3 After twenty-five years he finally *achieved* his ambition.
4 In English cinemas it's very *common* to have an ice-cream in the interval.
5 Have you got any *room* in your car for me?
6 I'd like two tickets for the Saturday evening performance – preferably two *seats* next to the *aisle*.

13 *READER ACTIVITY*

If upper-intermediate or advanced students were given the words below, they would probably encounter a number of pronunciation difficulties unless the words were known to them. However, some of the words are likely to be more difficult than others. (For the moment, we are putting aside the difficulties likely to be encountered by different nationalities (e.g. German /v/ and /w/, Japanese /l/ and /r/) and we are focussing on the problems of sound/spelling relationships common to *most* learners.)

1 Can you decide which words would create most problems?
2 What skills are necessary for a student to improve his pronunciation?

vicarage	sew
tomb	rectory
deniable	thyme
phrenology	awry
wrestle	bough
knave	dough

14 *READER ACTIVITY*

What changes, if any, would you wish to make to the language employed in the passages below, and what particular feature of vocabulary teaching do they highlight?

1 *On the telephone:*
Mrs Jones: Hello?
Carlo: Uh, is that Mrs Jones?
Mrs Jones: Yes.
Carlo: Oh, Mrs Jones, this is Carlo. I'm phoning because I'm going to the cinema after school so I'll be absent for dinner.
Mrs Jones: O.K. Carlo, that's fine. What time shall I see you, then?
Carlo: I think I'll arrive home at approximately ten o'clock. ⟫→

2 *Memo from the Managing Director to company employees:*
It has come to our attention that certain employees are smoking in the workshop. We must remind you that this is in contravention of the fire regulations and the Health and Safety Act 1978, and failure to observe this rule could land the company in a lot of trouble. We would appreciate your full co-operation in this matter.

3 *In a host family:*
John: Hey, Hiroshi, you can't possibly work with that noise going on downstairs.
Hiroshi: Yes, it is rather loud.
John: Well, I'll go and tell them to turn the record player down a bit.
Hiroshi: No, don't disturb yourself, I'll endure it.

4 *In a shop:*
Shop assistant: Is there anything else I can get you, love?
Young foreign student: No thank you, my dear.

5 *Taken from a job reference:*
Since his promotion, Mr Roberts has made great strides. Not only has he reorganised the distribution network fantastically well, but he has also demonstrated considerable flair for managerial responsibility. I believe that if he keeps this up, he will soon become a terrific Sales Manager, and I would recommend him for this position without any reservations.

6 *A landlady talking to a foreign student who is studying in England and staying at her house:*
Landlady: What are you doing this evening, Klaus?
Klaus: I have a meeting with a class colleague in a pub.

---

15 *READER ACTIVITY*

Read the two articles which follow and decide:
a) What is the difference between the two passages?
b) What is the effect of this difference?

1 A RIPPER victim said yesterday her £20,000 compensation means nothing.

Teresa Sykes declared, "The cash cannot solve my problems."

The payout is the highest ever awarded to anyone who survived an attack by murderer Peter Sutcliffe.

But nothing can erase the memory of three years ago when Teresa was hit on the head by Sutcliffe with a hammer.

Teresa, 19, said: "It's always worse when I am in bed. I'm so scared I sleep with a breadknife under my pillow."

The severity of the attack left her in hospital with serious head injuries. She was there for two months. But as the physical scars healed, the emotional problems deepened.

2

TORMENT OF RIPPER GIRL

'£20,000 cannot end my nightmare'

By CLIVE HADFIELD

A RIPPER victim said yesterday her £20,000 compensation "means nothing."

Teresa Sykes declared: "The cash cannot end my nightmare."

The payout is the highest ever awarded to anyone who survived attack by mass murderer Peter Sutcliffe.

But nothing can erase the nightmare of three years ago when Teresa was smashed in the head by the hammer-wielding killer.

Teresa—keeps knife

· *Teresa, 19, said: "It's always worse when I am in bed. I'm so scared I sleep with a bread knife under my pillow."*

The savagery of the attack left her in hospital with horrific head injuries.

She was there for two months. But as the physical scars healed, the emotional torment deepened.

She broke off her engagement to 28-year-old Jimmy Furey—the man who saved her.

Jimmy, the father of Teresa's two young children, saw Sutcliffe pounce near her home in Huddersfield, West Yorkshire, and scared him off.

Teresa said: "Marriage is out of the question. I'd always be worried that a husband would be violent towards me.

"When I go out it is with a group and even then I am always looking over my shoulder."

The £20,000 was awarded by the Criminal Injuries Compensation Board. Sutcliffe is now serving life for 13 killings.

Teresa added: "What he did to me made me a different person. No amount of money can compensate me."

(from the *Sunday Mirror*)

11

16 <u>*READER ACTIVITY*</u>

The following tapescript is from an authentic radio advertisement for a
brand of British wine. Underline the socio-cultural references in it which
you imagine foreign learners would not understand:
e.g. 'Wapping' in line 3 is a traditionally run-down area of London dockland
where you would not expect a yacht to be moored.

Daphne's Diary – the Diary of an upper-crust lady.

Dear Diary,
Thursday found me down on the Riviera – the S.S. Riviera – Lord Willoughby's yacht – moored at Wapping. Lord Willoughby, a man of
great refinement, arrived with bottles of the refreshing, light 'Concorde'
– in his rubber dinghy.
Lord Willboughby: Excuse me, but mind my inflatable with that boat-
hook!
(Sound of air escaping and dinghy sinking)
Daphne: We managed to save both the red and the white Concorde,
and as a bonus, Bobo was found clutching a bottle of rosé. I don't
mind telling you, dear Diary, as I leant against the cabin door, sipping
my delicious glass of Concorde, I found it . . .
(loud splashing noise – scream – Daphne falls in the water)
. . . most refreshing!

Concorde – the taste that rises to any occasion.

2   Words and their meanings

2.1   Conceptual meaning

If a group of language learners are shown three or four examples of a drinking vessel and told that each one is a 'cup', they will quickly establish some of the features that constitute a 'cup' in English. Indeed, for most learners this will simply involve attaching a new name to a familiar object for which there is an equivalent word in their own language, so recognising and naming other cups on subsequent occasions should not, in principle, be difficult. However, unlike a word such as 'sun' or 'moon', which refers to a single fixed entity, 'cup' is relatively indeterminate in meaning. Subtle differences in material, shape or function are all sufficient for the object to cease being a cup (in English). Languages rarely divide up the world in exactly the same way, and so we should not be surprised if we find students using the word 'cup' to describe an object which is in fact a 'glass', a 'mug' or even a 'bowl'. Even students whose mother tongue categorises this group of objects in the same way as English, cannot be sure that this is the case until they have learnt it. To understand a word fully, therefore, a student must know not only what it refers to, but also where the boundaries are that separate it from words of related meaning.

READER ACTIVITY

The words below can all be illustrated by ostensive definition (i.e. by pointing to the object itself), yet learned in isolation they could still be confused at a later date with words of related meaning. In each case, think of another word or words that are clearly similar to and yet distinct from the item given, and define the distinction:

e.g. sink   *washbasin*
      distinction: largely one of function and location i.e. sinks are found in kitchens and used for washing dishes and pans, while washbasins are found in bathrooms and used for personal hygiene.

suitcase   T-shirt
brochure   advertisement
dustbin

POLYSEMY

The importance of recognising the boundaries between lexical items is further illustrated by a brief look at polysemy. We use this term to describe a single word form with several different but closely related meanings. In English for example, we can talk about the 'head' of a person, the 'head' of a pin, or the 'head' of an organisation. Knowing that a single word denotes a particular set of things in one language is, however, no guarantee that it will denote the same set of things in another language. A Spanish student complaining of a problem on one of the fingers of his foot is probably neither a contortionist nor physically deformed, but simply guilty of the erroneous assumption that *dedos* (fingers) will denote the appendages to the hands and feet in English as it does in Spanish. Unfortunately for him we have two different words. An English student learning Portuguese might encounter the same problem in the assumption that the Portuguese word *janela* (window) can be used in the same contexts as it is in English. In Portuguese, however, a window in a house is called a *janela* but a window in a shop is called a *vitrine*.

READER ACTIVITY

Complete the following examples of polysemy in English. If you are a non-native speaker of English, note the degree to which they correspond with your own language. Native speakers might consider these examples in relation to a foreign language with which they are familiar.

e.g.   leg   *of a person/chair*
      mouth   *of a person/...*
      branch   *of a tree/...*
      top
      tail

HOMONYMY

When a single word form has several different meanings which are not closely related, we use the term homonymy e.g. a file /faɪl/ may be used for keeping papers in, or it may be a tool for cutting or smoothing hard substances. This absence of relatedness makes homonymy less of a problem, although at a receptive level misunderstanding can still arise as shown by the following exchange which we overheard:

    Teacher: If you go to a football match in England it's better to buy
            a stand ticket.
    Student: Yes, OK, but is it possible to sit as well?

Strictly speaking, this is an example of partial homonymy, as the confusion arises from the different meanings of a word when used in a different grammatical form i.e. 'stand' as a noun and verb. Nevertheless it is perplexing to find that the noun denotes that part of a stadium that is usually covered and furnished with seats, in apparent contradiction to the meaning of the verb.

SYNONYMY

Another difficulty with meaning arises with groups of words that share a general sense and so may be interchangeable in a limited number of contexts, but which on closer inspection reveal conceptual differences. Consider the following sentence:

The company has decided to extend its range of products.

The general sense of 'extend' here is to enlarge or make bigger, and in this context the word could be replaced by 'increase' or 'expand'. Now look at the following examples:

We are going to | *extend*
increase the kitchen by ten feet this year.
expand

We want to | extend
increase our sales by ten per cent next year.
expand

The metal will | extend
increase if we heat it.
expand

In these examples only the italicised verb is correct, and diagrammatically we could illustrate a refinement to the general sense of enlargement in the following way:

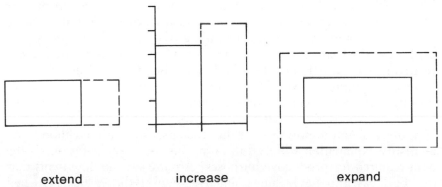

extend   increase   expand

In practice these notions of enlargement are still variable and there remain overlapping areas, particularly in the case of 'extend' versus 'increase', and 'increase' versus 'expand'.

15

Words: their meanings and forms

READER ACTIVITY

For each pair of words below, think of a context in which the items are interchangeable and a context in which only one of the words can be used:
e.g. refuse/reject

a) I'm afraid they | refused
   | rejected our offer.

b) We reject goods that do not meet the required standard.

target/goal
shallow/superficial
fetch/bring
to rush/to hurry
think/believe

Words may also be ostensibly identical in meaning yet have a different reference. 'Umpires' and 'referees' perform identical tasks but whereas cricket and tennis have umpires, most other sports have referees. And why should lawn tennis be played on a court and football on a pitch?

One of the most exasperating examples of this for learners of English concerns the numeral '0', as can be seen from the following:

My phone number is six *o*/əʊ/ two seven.

Italy beat Spain two *nil* in the football match.

You must subtract *nought* point seven.

It was ten degrees below *zero* in Canada yesterday.

John McEnroe is leading forty *love* in this game. (tennis)

Teaching implications

The problems outlined in the preceding section may seem to present teachers with an extremely daunting task. If learners can only achieve a clear and comprehensive understanding of a lexical item through an exhaustive analysis of the conceptual boundaries that separate it from related items, teachers may be wondering when they will find the time to teach anything but vocabulary. In practice, there has to be a compromise, and before embarking on a lengthy analysis the teacher must first be convinced that the time will be well spent. For example: is the item of particular importance for the students? Is there a likelihood that a cursory explanation will lead to immediate or later confusion? Is the item required for productive purposes? Are the surrounding items that may be drawn into the teaching point also useful? If the teacher is satisfied that none of these questions will yield a positive answer, he should not feel guilty about glossing over some of the features of the item that may be essential for effective productive use. Returning to an earlier

16

example, it does seem appropriate with beginners or elementary students to teach 'glass' alongside 'cup'. Both items are likely to be useful productive items, and their conceptual similarity makes it imperative that the distinction between them is clearly drawn. 'Mug' on the other hand, is a lower frequency item and the meaning is quite adequately covered by a knowledge of 'cup'. Time spent refining the concepts and highlighting the differences is therefore unnecessary.

The position we have taken with regard to 'cup' and 'mug' reflects the widely held view that lower levels should be spared lexis that is superfluous to immediate need, or involves conceptual difficulties that may not easily be conveyed without using language of comparable complexity. Translation is obviously one way round the problem of explaining difficult concepts, although a suitable mother-tongue equivalent is not always available and the teacher may be forced into lengthy mother-tongue explanations to clarify a concept. For important items this is justifiable, but there is the danger of the lessons being dominated by the mother tongue; in the long term this may not be a desirable development. We will be returning to this subject in more detail in part B.

Without translation at their disposal, teachers would certainly be wise to give careful consideration to abstract items before entering into lengthy and possibly futile explanations. Unfortunately it is unrealistic to try and extend this protection to a point where elementary students are only exposed to concrete unambiguous items. Learners will almost certainly require conceptually difficult vocabulary to meet their own language needs, regardless of whether they are beginners or extremely advanced. Items such as 'training' and 'experience' are potentially very difficult for certain nationalities but may well be essential lexis at a very low level, particularly with business students. When these situations occur, teachers should not be worried about giving an item the detailed attention it deserves, and neither should they feel guilty about making the best possible use of bilingual dictionaries.

If you decide that an item does not warrant serious attention your teaching should still be informed by an awareness of the potential problems. The students may be quite satisfied with a quick mime to illustrate 'shiver', but you should not be surprised if they then 'shiver' with 'fear' or 'excitement' in their compositions. Had the possible confusion with 'tremble' and 'shake' been anticipated, these student errors could have been avoided by the briefest of explanations. Anticipating the problems though, is not easy, and there is no substitute for the classroom experience that enables teachers to know when and where problems are likely to occur. Dictionaries offer some guidance, although a more effective reference source is often the *Longman Lexicon of Contemporary English*, as it groups items within semantic fields and so brings together words that may well have conceptual similarities. First Certificate and Proficiency course books are another useful source, not because they necessarily solve the problems for you, but they do at least draw attention to many areas of common confusion.

2.2 Affective meaning

We are using this term to cover the attitudinal and emotional factors which can be expressed in an item of vocabulary. These are often referred to as *connotation*. '... An apparent synonym may on examination prove to have a similar or identical *denotation* but a different *connotation*. That is to say, it may have reference to an identical object or action, but the emotional or other overtones attached to its use may differ.' (Palmer, 1976)

For instance, 'Joanna is *a single woman*' differs from 'Joanna is *a spinster*' in that 'spinster' has a series of evaluative and emotional associations for an English native speaker which would not be true of 'single woman'. These associations may include old, isolated, on the shelf, a sad figure, etc.; in other words, hardly complimentary. The conceptual meaning of both items is, however, identical i.e. an unmarried adult female.

When we examine lexical items from the learner's point of view, we can identify three main areas of connotation which are likely to be of interest.

Firstly, certain items intrinsically have a positive or negative connotation. 'Complacent' invariably carries a negative connotation, so the statement 'I find him very complacent' can really only be interpreted as a criticism. Being described as 'dogmatic' or 'naïve' is equally unflattering because of the negative connotations involved. Teachers will need to highlight this aspect of meaning, particularly in cases where the conceptual meaning alone does not make explicit the attitudinal force of a word.

The second area of connotation involves items which vary in affective meaning depending on the speaker's attitude or the situation. Our understanding of the same item used by different speakers or the same speaker in different contexts may change radically.

One area in which this form of personal expression is very common is in social groupings and political language. Look at the following sentences and compare the use of the word 'liberal'.

a) It's probably the most liberal régime in an area rife with dictatorships.
b) I find the Thatcher government's policy on immigration far too liberal.
c) He's a typical liberal – says he supports the pay claim, but he won't come out on strike with us.

The speaker in (a) is using 'liberal' in a positive sense, whereas in (b) and (c) both speakers are using the word pejoratively, albeit from politically different points of view. In other words, the affective meaning of an item can vary according to the context and speaker.

Thirdly, *socio-cultural associations* of lexical items are a further area of difficulty for foreign learners. Native speakers of a language have a whole series of associations with certain items and these associations are common to the society as a whole. Ask a British native speaker what he associates with 'Friday the 13th' and he will almost certainly say bad luck, broken mirrors, walking under ladders and will list other such superstitions. These associations are extremely unlikely in many countries, though in some countries 'Tuesday the 13th' might trigger a similar series of associations. These are examples of socio-culturally specific concepts; parts of the way of life of a culture which may or may not be shared by foreigners.

Proper names and place names may well cause learners great problems (see 'Daphne's Diary' – ch. 1, activity 16) and food, drink, clothes and traditions have strong cultural associations. Within these areas, however, there are still likely to be variations of association from person to person. While nearly every British English speaker would associate Agatha Christie with Hercule Poirot and thrillers, some people's associations would also include 'a good read on a winter's evening', others would think of unsophisticated style or class prejudice.

Teaching implications

It is obvious that many items only have a conceptual meaning and in normal use have no emotional or evaluative associations attached to them. However, where an item has emotional or evaluative associations, we need to clarify this for learners. Since connotation is a feature common to every language, students will not find the process new, but will need to appreciate which items have added affective meaning over and above their conceptual meaning, and whether these are fixed or vary according to context.

Text work (i.e. reading and listening activities) is the most obvious vehicle for dealing with this aspect of vocabulary teaching, since a real context is essential. Even then, the information provided in the text may not be fully adequate.

At low levels, teachers and materials writers normally present items which are of immediate use to students. In the majority of cases, these items do not have strong emotional or evaluative associations. Students of a higher level will be expected to deal with a range of spoken and written language and this will demand an understanding of connotation. However, it may well be of interest or relevance to a low level student to appreciate the connotations of certain 'cognates' and to compare the difference, for example, between an item such as 'radical' in their own culture with the same item in American or British culture. A contrastive approach and the use of the mother tongue may be very suitable in these circumstances.

While teachers are often able to make a conscious decision about the cultural content of their syllabus, there are many situations in which this is prescribed by either the course book or the circumstances. An awareness of the level of difficulty of cultural references in a piece of material will help a teacher to determine whether or not it is worth selecting; in many teaching contexts, culturally-bound materials and themes may be rejected. However, when learners are in an English-speaking environment or are intending to go to one, the teacher is obliged to deal with cultural associations to help the learner survive in the community. So while in his own country a learner's life will probably not be affected by not knowing who the Prime Minister of Great Britain is, the learner in Britain who does not know such things may fail to understand many everyday references around him.

If a teacher were to use material such as 'Daphne's Diary' (in ch. 1) – admittedly this is a very extreme example, and would not be appropriate in a lot of teaching situations – it would be possible to make the material more accessible and comprehensible by examining class attitudes and British humour with the group beforehand. Ultimately, the success of the handling of this whole area depends on the teacher's sensitivity to the group's level and needs as well as his awareness of the connotations and associations of target items.

2.3   Style, register and dialect

Some of the more amusing errors a learner can make in a foreign language arise from a lack of awareness of the appropriacy of items. We gave some examples of this type in chapter 1, and include a few here:

Teacher: Are you going out this evening, Giovanni?
Italian student: No, I have to wash my underlinen.

Female teacher (walking into class): Hello, everyone.
Students: Hello.
Male student: Hi, baby.

Student: The post office is yonder, I think.

We are using *style* in a very broad sense to include level of formality (i.e. slang, colloquial or informal, neutral, formal, frozen) as well as styles such as humorous, ironic, poetic, literary, etc. The following items are similar in conceptual meaning but differ in style:

children (neutral)
offspring (formal, sometimes humorous)
nippers (colloquial, often humorous)
kids (colloquial)
brats (colloquial, derogatory)

Registers are varieties of language defined by their topic and context of use; the language of medicine, education, law, computers, etc. come into this category:
e.g. 'minor' is the legal term for 'child'
'insolvent' is the banking term for 'penniless'
'cardiac arrest' is the medical term for 'heart attack'

Dialect is used to describe differences in geographical variation (e.g. American English, Scottish English, etc.) as well as variation according to social class. We need not concern ourselves greatly with the latter. Geographical dialectal variety, on the other hand, will produce contrasts such as
sidewalk (US) = pavement (GB)
wee (Scottish colloquial) = small (GB)
G'day (Australian) = Hello (GB)

READER ACTIVITY

With each of the following items, indicate any remarkable features of style, register or dialect:
e.g. faucet: *neutral, US*

1 emoluments	6 loo
2 cosine	7 communicative competence
3 a shrink	8 bonkers
4 hence	9 bairn
5 to fancy something	

Teaching implications

Style, register and dialect strongly affect the impression we gain of a learner's competence in the language, and this is shown, amongst other things, in his choice of lexis. It is quite common for native speakers to be surprised at the level of apparent formality of foreign speakers, and there are particular problems for speakers of Romance languages through mother-tongue interference:
e.g. 'There isn't *sufficient* milk for breakfast', where the speaker simply means 'not enough'.

It can be equally surprising for native speakers to hear foreigners using colloquial language which is either inappropriate (as in 'hi, baby') or

21

which sounds distinctly odd unless the foreigner is an extremely competent speaker.

Although stylistic appropriacy is clearly important, low level general English learners have a particular need for vocabulary items with wide coverage; items which are not neutral are likely to be more specialised and perhaps of less immediate value to a beginner. At later levels, it may become necessary for learners to acquire a knowledge of a variety of styles, and a particular register or dialect appropriate to their present or future needs. The teacher's role here is to select language items carefully and highlight any special features for the learner. Some EFL dictionaries can be useful in this respect to both teachers and learners as they often indicate all three aspects. (We recommend that you proceed cautiously, however; 'brat' on p. 21 is listed in both the *Longman Dictionary of Contemporary English (LDCE)* and the *Oxford Advanced Learner's Dictionary of Current English (OALDCE)* but no indication is given of the colloquial nature of this item.) Bilingual dictionaries are often a notorious source of deception in this area.

Style particularly will affect all learners, although the decision to teach certain stylistic values for productive use must be governed by students' needs. Colloquial language, slang or literary style, for instance, may be of value receptively to many learners; this would be particularly true in the case of colloquial language for students learning in an English-speaking country. They will need to be able to respond appropriately to such utterances as:

> Do you fancy a drink?
> Can I have a ciggy?

However, productively these items have very limited use for all but the most competent speakers. It is also worth remembering that many learners need English to converse with other foreigners, and in such cases, a more neutral style will be more useful.

There is a great deal of completely unjustified snobbery surrounding certain *dialects* of English. Whether a student should learn 'boot' of a car (GB), or 'trunk' of a car (US), or both, is governed by the people with whom he will wish to communicate. On the whole, though, dialect is not a major issue in vocabulary teaching. Students who are learning their English for specific purposes will, of course, need vocabulary of particular *registers* e.g. medical, banking, legal, etc.

2.4 Sense relations

The meaning of a word can only be understood and learnt in terms of its relationship with other words in the language. In our native language, we can easily identify the relationships between words; we know that:

'Revolting' can be a synonym for 'disgusting' in certain contexts.

'Sharp' is the antonym for 'blunt' in certain contexts.

'Hatchet', 'pickaxe' and 'chopper' are all *types* of axe, and can be sharp or blunt.

If Bernard is Jeff's 'employee', then Jeff is Bernard's 'employer'.

In this section, we will explore these and other sense relations in greater depth.

2.4.1 SYNONYMY

Earlier in the chapter we discussed several examples of conceptual synonymy, or rather, partial conceptual synonymy e.g. umpire/referee, and increase/extend/expand. It is rarely the case that two words will be synonymous on every occasion – if they were, there would be little need to have both words in the language. So, when we use the term synonymy we are actually talking about partial synonymy, and the following examples illustrate how synonymy may differ:

flat = apartment different dialect i.e. GB versus US
kid = child different style i.e. colloquial versus neutral
skinny = thin different connotation i.e. 'skinny' is more pejorative
conceal = hide as transitive verbs, but 'hide' may also be intransitive, thus different grammar

As long as these differences are highlighted, the use of synonyms is often a quick and efficient way of explaining unknown words. A more complex classroom example than the ones above involves synonyms with collocational restrictions. The verb 'commit' may be defined as 'do' or 'make' in the examples to 'commit a crime' or 'commit an error', but it would need to be pointed out that 'commit' only collocates with certain nouns and is not generally synonymous with 'do' or 'make'. This area is dealt with more fully on page 37.

READER ACTIVITY

For each of the italicised words in the text we have suggested two synonyms. Choose the best one in each case and decide if the synonym needs to be qualified in any way.

A recent *poll* (1) revealed that many parents felt there was too much violence on TV. Interestingly enough, only eight per cent felt that sex was more *harmful* (2) than violence.

What emerged most clearly from the mass of figures was that parents exercise little control over their childrens' viewing, even when it worries them. They put the *onus* (3) on the programme makers which is both irresponsible and unfair. Although I am against censorship, the survey convinces me that there should be some sort of indication given to parents as to the suitability of programmes. Even if children cannot be prevented from watching television, at least there could be a warning before the programme starts if it includes scenes likely to upset *minors* (4). This already happens in America.

Personally I would like to attach a warning to all those *nasty* (5), *smutty* (6) comedy shows. However, when I suggested that to a number of TV programme producers I was accused of being *biased* (7) – such are the problems of setting oneself up as a censor.

(adapted from *Themes*)

1 survey/investigation	5 unpleasant/vicious
2 damaging/noxious	6 dirty/filthy
3 responsibility/blame	7 prejudiced/subjective
4 children/youngsters	

2.4.2 HYPONYMY

It would not be accurate to say that 'fruit' equals 'orange', but we can say that the meaning of 'fruit' is included in the meaning of 'orange', as it is in the meaning of 'apple', 'pear' and 'plum'. We express this sense relation by saying that 'fruit' is a superordinate and that 'orange', 'apple', 'pear' and 'plum' are all hyponyms of 'fruit'. In the same way, 'cow', 'horse', 'pig' and 'dog' are all hyponyms of the superordinate 'animal'. Thus:

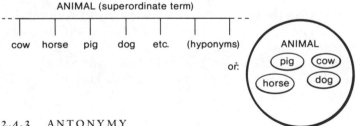

2.4.3 ANTONYMY

There are a variety of different forms of 'oppositeness' which are relevant to learners and teachers; these include *complementarity, converseness, multiple taxonomy* and *gradable antonymy*. We feel that it is worth examining these relations in greater depth as they may help to highlight the difficulties students sometimes experience if they are asked the ubiquitous question, 'What's the opposite of . . .?'

Note that not all linguists use the same terminology to describe the semantic relations which follow, and alternative terminology has therefore been included in brackets.

24

Complementaries (also 'binary antonyms' or 'binary taxonomy')
These are forms of antonyms which truly represent oppositeness of meaning. They cannot be graded (cf. *gradable antonyms* below) and if one of the pair is applicable, then the other cannot be. They are said to be mutually exclusive:
e.g. X is *male*   Y is *female*

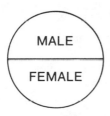

If a human being or animal is male, then clearly it cannot be female. This is a clear-cut area of opposition and a 'safe' one for the very common teacher's question, 'What's the opposite of ...?'

READER ACTIVITY

What are the complementaries of the following?

1 dead   4 animate
2 true   5 imperfect
3 same

Converses
With certain pairs of lexical items, there is another form of 'oppositeness', called converseness, and two examples follow:
1 a) Julia is Martin's *wife*.
  b) Martin is Julia's *husband*.
2 a) The picture is *above* the fireplace.
  b) The fireplace is *below* the picture.

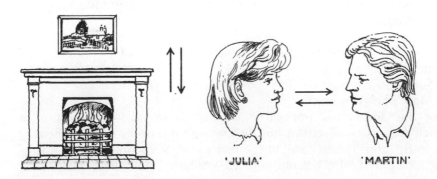

In the examples above, (a) and (b) paraphrase each other, and we can see the relationship between the pairs as being reciprocal. Family and social relations provide many examples of converses, as do space and time relations.

Transform the sentences below as in the examples above.

1 Tom is Mary's brother.
Mary is ...
2 David is Margaret's nephew.
Margaret is ...
3 John is taller than Nigel.
Nigel is ...
4 John Walker is my doctor.
I'm ...
5 Bill sold Tom a tractor.
Tom ...
6 John owns that blue Toyota.
That blue Toyota ...
7 The geography lesson came after the film.
The film ...

You will notice that in the above exercise, we were unable to ask you to give the *opposites*; had we done so, we would have been forced to accept 'doesn't own' as the opposite of 'own', for example. While there are many cases where the technique of asking for opposites would be clear and effective, there are obviously cases, especially where no context is given, when confusion can arise. A teacher who asks, 'What's the opposite of "children"?' might be given the answer 'adults' or 'parents' and both would be fully justifiable. With converses, therefore, it is safer to define clearly and the following technique is useful:

Sue and Jon are Charlotte and David's *parents* so David and Charlotte are ...

Some of these converses may not transfer to other languages. Family relations are a notorious minefield where, for example, in Spanish, *hermanos* may mean 'brothers' or 'brothers and sisters', and 'cousin' has a masculine and feminine form. Another common problem occurs with 'borrow' and 'lend', and for a learner whose language does not have two lexical equivalents, there may be great difficulty in visualising this sense relationship.

Gradable antonyms (also 'gradable opposites', 'polar opposites' and 'antonyms')

Sue's house is *big*.

Mary's house is *small*.

Are 'big' and 'small' opposites? Most of us would use opposition to teach these two adjectives, but they are not opposites in the same way as 'male' and 'female' are. In the first place, Sue's house is 'relatively' big, compared with her old house, considering how many people live with her, in relation to her income and status; Mary's house may be 'relatively' small in the light of the same factors. In fact, Sue and Mary might live in identical houses next door to each other, but the sentences are obviously subjective and depend on the speaker's opinion. Secondly, 'big' and 'small' form part of a scale of values which will include some of the following:

NORM/AVERAGE
huge/very big/BIG/quite big/medium-sized/ quite small/SMALL/tiny

Another feature of gradable antonyms is that with many examples, particularly to do with size and age, only one of the pair is commonly used as the 'unmarked' term e.g. 'How *long* is the room?' (not 'How short is it?') 'It's six metres *long*' (not 'six metres short'). This is the case with antonyms such as old/young, old/new, high/low, etc.

<hr>

READER ACTIVITY

To each of the following gradable antonyms add the rest of the scale, as in the example above for 'big' and 'small'.

1 hot/cold (water) 3 interesting/boring (a film)
2 love/hate 4 good/bad (a book)

Multiple incompatibles (also 'multiple taxonomy')

These are sets of miniature semantic systems which are of interest to teachers and learners as they are easily memorable, and many (though not all) occur in other languages. Some of these are closed systems (i.e. having a strictly limited number) while others are open systems (i.e. covering a much wider field, often an indeterminate number). Here are some examples of 'closed' systems:

spring	summer
autumn	winter

Monday
Tuesday
Wednesday
Thursday
Friday
Saturday
Sunday

Using one item from the set excludes all the others in the same system.

27

Add the rest of the system to the items below.

1 liquid (system of three)   4 Earth (system of nine)
2 hearts (system of four)   5 earth (system of four)
3 indigo (system of seven)   6 breakfast (system of three or four?)

Here are some examples of 'open-ended' systems. These are, of course, further examples of superordinates and hyponyms.
   Vehicles: car, bus, lorry, van, etc.
   Flowers: lily, daffodil, pansy, geranium, etc.
   Tools: screwdriver, hammer, saw, chisel, etc.

2.4.4   OTHER TYPES OF RELATIONS

There are further sets of relations between items which are less easily definable but have to do with *cause and effect*. The reason for their importance in language learning is that these relationships may offer vital clues when learners are unfamiliar with items and need to guess from context. Also exploited here is the learner's knowledge of the world, and we would stress the need to acquire a good understanding of connectives (see p. 70).

   In the two examples below, 'mop' and 'lawnmower' may not be familiar to the learner. Arrows have been drawn to show the notional relations he can exploit to help him deduce the meaning of the unknown word.

The (floor's) really (dirty) ; can you give it (a wash) with the (mop)?

Can we borrow your lawnmower? Ours has broken and the (grass) has got terribly (long).

In addition, there are paired sets which express *directional* opposition e.g. up/down, arrive/depart, come/go.

Part–whole relations
The following diagram is an example of a type of sense relation which is much used in language classrooms.

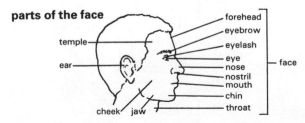

parts of the face

forehead
eyebrow
temple
eyelash
ear
eye
nose   face
nostril
mouth
chin
cheek jaw   throat

This differs from hyponomy in that while a cow is a kind of animal, an eyebrow is not a kind of face but *part* of the face.

Items commonly associated with ...

With this type of relation we are drawing on our knowledge of the world. Ask a native speaker what items he commonly associates with 'kitchen' and he will probably list the appliances, gadgets and general

contents illustrated in the picture above. Although a certain amount of individual variation is inevitable, the lists compiled by native speakers of the same language are likely to be similar. There is, however, the possibility of sometimes quite dramatic discrepancies from culture to culture. Few British kitchens have waffle irons, and few Argentinian kitchens contain kettles.

2.4.5 TRANSLATION EQUIVALENTS

For language learners, there is a further type of sense relation, that is the relationship between a lexical item in English and the nearest mother-tongue equivalent. Most learners find it useful to make a conscious effort to link words between languages in this way and in the early stages of learning it is inevitable that they will do so. There are several types of translation equivalent, some of which may be a very straightforward form of literal translation (e.g. *L'encre* (French) = ink). However, many equivalents are only partially synonymous and teachers should be particularly sensitive to these differences if they are using translation in the classroom for vocabulary teaching. On the surface, some items appear to be similar, but there are often cultural differences. English 'bread' neither looks nor tastes like *pain* in France, *Brot* in Germany or *pão* in Portugal. It is also quite common to find that equivalents do not even exist; the 'cup', 'mug' and 'bowl' discussed at the beginning of the chapter do not translate into three separate words in Chinese, for instance. Sometimes languages will 'borrow' words from each other to help deal with this (as in the case of 'wok' in English) but it is equally common for this borrowing to take place for stylistic purposes (e.g. *le smoking* in French, 'chauffeur' in English). It is often the case that proverbs and sayings cannot be translated literally; the French equivalent of 'a bull in a china shop' is 'a dog in a game of skittles'.

A second type of problem occurs when the meaning of an item in one context is identical in both languages but where there are grammatical differences. The verb 'to depend (on something/somebody)' for instance, provokes errors of translation such as 'it depends of him'. Nouns such as 'luggage' which are uncountable in English but countable in some other languages also cause difficulty. A similar example of transposition would be *Défense de Fumer*, *Prohibido Fumar* and 'No Smoking' where syntactic preferences will dictate the equivalents.

READER ACTIVITY

Sense relations: a practical exercise.

When presenting, checking understanding or testing language items, it is common to use the questions below.

Box A

What's the opposite of . . .?

What's the | masculine form of . . .?
| feminine

What's missing from this group?

What's another | word for . . .?
| way of saying . . .?

Sentence completion e.g. Tom is Henry's uncle so John . . .?

What's the difference between . . .?

(e.g. What's the difference between 'to kill someone' and 'to do someone
  in'?
  'To kill' is neutral, 'to do someone in' is very colloquial.)

Now look at the lexical items in box B:

Box B

a) waitress   g) a wide road
b) to pass an exam   h) to rent
c) a knife   i) army
d) to own   j) gasoline
e) to sell   k) cardiac arrest
f) in front of   l) awful

---

1 For each of the items above in box B, decide which other item(s) you might
  wish to check or teach against the known item:
  e.g. (a) waitress   *Answer:* waiter, or perhaps customer.
2 Now choose one of the questions or techniques suggested in box A which
  you feel would be most effective and appropriate to elicit the items in
  box B.
  You may find more than one way of eliciting the item, though sometimes
  different questions will elicit different answers:

  e.g. waiter–waitress
  Q: What's the feminine form of 'waiter'?
  e.g. waitress–customer
  Q: In a restaurant, the customer is served by the waiter or . . .

Sense relations: teaching implications

In language learning and teaching, sense relations are of paramount
importance. In the classroom, grouping items together by synonymy,
hyponymy, antonymy and other types of relations will help to give coher-
ence to the lesson. As a means of presentation and testing, these relationships are extremely valuable, and can provide a useful framework for

the learner to understand semantic boundaries: to see where meaning overlaps and learn the limits of use of an item. Their usefulness in terms of organisation clearly extends beyond the classroom; as a coherent record for the student they are very effective. A variety of forms of storage are suggested in part B.

One final but extremely important function of sense relations is that they help us to make deductions about unknown items. The examples below illustrate how vital sense relations are in contextual guesswork. In each case, the item in italics is assumed to be unknown to the learner.

The village had most of the usual *amenities*: a pub, a library, post office, village hall, medical centre and school.

You may wish to make explicit to the learner how, in this case, the superordinate term ('amenities') signals the examples of the type which follow. The punctuation is also an important clue here. The following examples could be used in a similar way:

Co-educational schools (i.e. mixed sex schools) are more common than they used to be. (synonym)

He was incredibly untidy; the bed was covered in a pile of trousers, shirts, ties, socks and *underwear*. (hyponym)

I expected him to be very hard-working but in fact he was very *idle*. (antonym)

He passed me a knife so that I could *carve* the meat. (notional relation)

Visual aids, diagrams and trees which make sense relations explicit are also a helpful teaching and learning device and examples of these are given earlier in this chapter (the kitchen vocabulary on page 29 and the parts of the face on page 28). Further examples are given in the section on written storage in chapter 6. With gradable antonyms, a line similar to the one on page 108 can be given to the learners. Some of the items can be listed at the bottom for the students to put in the appropriate place. This not only provides a useful framework but is a record for the students too. With text work, students can be asked to underline the items which have some kind of sense relationship, such as all the items associated with driving. They could also be asked to find antonyms in a text for a given list of adjectives. Another way of introducing items is to give students a list of co-hyponyms:

carve   pare   dice   slice   trim

and ask students to find out how they are related by using their dictionaries. (In the case above, the *OALDCE* includes the word 'cut' in all the definitions.)

We have seen how a clear understanding of sense relations can provide greater precision in guiding students towards meaning, and in helping them to define the boundaries that separate lexical items. It should also be evident that the ubiquitous classroom practice of saying 'it's the same as', or 'it's the opposite of', is not always an adequate explanation.

Carried to extremes this can erode credibility; if subsequent lessons constantly undermine the validity of previous explanations, the students may lose faith in their teacher. For this reason it is advisable to warn your students if you are using synonymy or antonymy loosely, and give your reasons. Telling the students that an 'excruciating' film means a 'terrible' film is perfectly acceptable if your aim is simply to convey a general understanding without causing an unnecessary digression in the lesson; it will probably allay their fears over the new item and allow you to pass over a low frequency item swiftly and conveniently.

2.5 Multi-word verbs

We are using this term to describe the large number of English verbs consisting of two, or sometimes three parts:
a) A 'base' verb + preposition e.g. look into (investigate), get over (recover from).
b) A 'base' verb + adverbial particle (phrasal verb) e.g. break down (collapse), call off (cancel).
c) A 'base' verb + adverbial particle + preposition e.g. put up with (tolerate).

As our examples illustrate, there are verb + preposition combinations which share with many phrasal verbs the fact that the meaning is not clear from the individual parts; this probably explains why certain grammar books and course writers include semantically opaque prepositional verbs in their treatment of phrasal verbs. In our experience the distinction does not pose a significant teaching problem, but if you wish to pursue the difference we would refer you to one of the grammar books listed in the bibliography. For our purposes we will use the term 'phrasal verb' when referring specifically to verb + adverbial particle, and multi-word verb to include semantically opaque prepositional verbs as well.

In some cases phrasal verbs retain the meaning of their individual verb and particle e.g. sit down, while in others the meaning cannot be deduced from an understanding of the constituent parts e.g. take in (deceive/cheat somebody). It is this latter category which creates most difficulty and contributes to the mystique which surrounds multi-word verbs for many foreign learners. Also contributing to the mystique is the fact that many phrasal verbs have multiple meaning e.g. pick up can mean lift, acquire, collect, etc.

Grammatically, students need to know whether a transitive multi-word verb is phrasal or prepositional. This is because phrasal verbs are separable:

e.g. take off your hat   take it off
    take your hat off   (but not 'take off it')

while prepositional verbs are not:
e.g. look after the children
        look after them
        (but not 'look the children after', 'look them after')
Finally, there is the question of style. Some common phrasal verbs are informal, and have one-word equivalents which are preferred in more formal contexts (e.g. put off / postpone; get along / manage). Students will need to be made aware of restrictions of this kind.

Teaching implications

We have already mentioned the obsession with multi-word verbs which seems to grip many foreign learners, particularly as they pass through the intermediate level. Unwittingly teachers and materials writers have contributed more than anyone to this irrational obsession by often ignoring multi-word verbs in the early stages of learning, only to unleash them in massive doses on students preparing for the Cambridge First Certificate Examination. Students are suddenly confronted with ten or fifteen different particles or prepositions accompanying 'put', or 'get', or 'take', with a seemingly infinite variety of meanings; no wonder they are confused.

In the opening chapter we included an exercise which raised the question of how to group multi-word verbs for teaching purposes, which in turn raises the question as to whether they should be grouped at all. As stated in the key, we see little reason to start from the root verb since the items will be largely unrelated in meaning. From the learner's point of view this does not help to make them memorable, and for the teacher further practice will be more difficult to organise. With regard to the similarity of form, we believe it is more confusing than it is constructive.

With some phrasal verbs there is justification in starting with the adverbial particle, as there are instances where the particle performs a fairly consistent function with regard to the influence on the root verb. A good example of this is 'off' which often implies a general sense of separation, more accurately described with various verbs as:

becoming detached   e.g. to break off
being removed   e.g. to take off
being disconnected   e.g. to turn off
departing   e.g. to set off
disappearing   e.g. to wear off

Further examples include the particle 'up' which often serves to emphasise the root verb and express a sense of completion e.g. do up, drink up, grow up; and 'on' which sometimes adds a sense of continuation to the main verb e.g. go on, carry on, keep on, drive on. This last group

34

of phrasal verbs could easily be presented together to a class of students and then practised through a speaking activity in which the students give directions to each other about how to get to their house or some other destination.

Where the meaning of a multi-word verb cannot be deduced from the individual parts, it is sensible to treat the item as one would any other item of vocabulary and apply the same criteria in either selecting it or rejecting it for teaching purposes. A probable outcome of this approach is that certain multi-word verbs e.g. turn on / turn off, will be introduced at a very early stage and more will be added at regular intervals thereafter. Initially one need only teach grammatical features as they apply to individual items, and then, when the students have encountered a number of different types of verb, a more systematic analysis of the grammar can be undertaken.

There will be occasions when a number of multi-word verbs within a single semantic field form a coherent group for teaching purposes, but this is seldom practicable. The danger is that the teacher is forced to include some low frequency items in order to form a worthwhile lexical set. A similar danger applies to tackling a phrasal verb in all its senses – tidy and comprehensive though this approach may be, different meanings of a phrasal verb rarely have equal usefulness for the students. Occasionally though, this may be a viable approach for revision purposes with advanced students.

Our reluctance to treat multi-word verbs in the classroom as a separate and independent lexical area (unless there is a very clear semantic or grammatical reason for doing so) should not be construed as an attempt to minimise their value. Used appropriately and accurately these verbs certainly contribute to a colloquial ease and fluency which is clearly a great asset. Equally, it should not be forgotten that many foreign learners will not use their English with native speakers but with other foreign learners who may neither use nor understand a wide range of multi-word verbs. Even foreign learners who do use their English with native speakers may find that these verbs, while being essential at a receptive level, are not a prerequisite for effective spoken English. The place and purpose of study is therefore an important factor in deciding the priority given to this area of vocabulary.

2.6 Idioms

An idiom is a sequence of words which operates as a single semantic unit, and like many multi-word verbs the meaning of the whole cannot be deduced from an understanding of the parts e.g. never mind, hang on, under the weather, etc. The other feature of idioms is that they are often syntactically restricted e.g. someone can have a 'chip on their shoulder', but not a 'shoulder with a chip'; and sometimes grammatically restricted e.g. you can have a 'white elephant', but the adjective cannot take the comparative form and become a 'whiter elephant'.

Although we have defined idioms as being semantically opaque we might also include in this section a wide range of expressions that are in fact deducible from the constituent parts. If, for example, we say that somebody is 'under pressure', our students should have no great difficulty in deducing the meaning, but they would be unlikely to generate the expression themselves from their prior knowledge of the individual words. The same could be said of 'first of all', 'to begin with', 'to make matters worse', and 'out of danger'. To this extent these expressions need to be consciously learned just as much as idioms that are semantically opaque.

Teaching implications

Many of the remarks we made about semantically opaque multi-word verbs will also be true of idioms. There is no sense in grouping them together on the basis of the individual words as they normally give little indication of the sense of the unit; and idioms rarely come in sufficient numbers at respective levels to warrant being a self-contained lexical set. In other words, they should be treated as individual items, taught as they arise, and emphasised according to their usefulness.

Some students develop an immense appetite and enthusiasm for idioms, but often for less useful types of idiom e.g. a wolf in sheep's clothing. When this happens teachers should try to channel this enthusiasm into learning idioms that are useful; and in deciding what is useful, it is worth considering whether an idiom can be incorporated into the students' productive vocabulary without seeming incongruous alongside the rest of their language. Certain native speakers might 'get the ball rolling', but few foreign learners could carry off this idiom without sounding faintly ridiculous.

The following activity is highly subjective but it might be interesting to compare your answers with your colleagues.

READER ACTIVITY

Which of the following items would you consider were worth teaching productively to a group of intermediate students? (*Note:* not all at the same time.)

tip of my tongue	sleep like a log
full of beans	it's up to you
fed up	get the sack

chip off the old block   pull somebody's leg
down in the dumps   make ends meet
raining cats and dogs   out of the blue

2.7 Collocation

When two items co-occur, or are used together frequently, they are said to collocate, and in chapter 1, activities 9 and 10, we gave examples of some of the collocational errors students are likely to commit. Items may co-occur simply because the combination reflects a common real world state of affairs. For instance, 'pass' and 'salt' collocate because people often want other people to pass them the salt. However, the collocations listed below have an added element of linguistic convention; English speakers have chosen to say, for example, that lions 'roar' rather than 'bellow'.

The most common types of collocation are as follows:

a) *subject noun + verb*   e.g. The *earth revolves* around the sun.
                                  The *lion roared.*
If we want to describe the movement of the earth in relation to the sun, then *'earth'* + *'revolve'* is a likely combination. It would be less common, for example, to use 'circulate'.

b) *verb + object noun*   e.g. She *bites* her *nails.*
On the whole, we would not use 'eat' here, though many other languages would.

c) *Adjective + noun*   e.g. a *loud noise, heavy traffic*
Notice how a different collocation (e.g. for 'noise', 'a big noise') would give an entirely different meaning.

d) *adverb + past participle used adjectivally*   e.g. *badly dressed, fully insured.*

Collocational grids are a useful way of clarifying the limits of items, and the grid on page 38 from *The Words You Need* (Rudska et al, 1981) relates to the componential analysis on page 41.

There are inevitably differences of opinion as to what represents an acceptable collocation in English. In the example below, we feel that 'a beautiful proposal', 'pretty furniture' and 'a lovely bird' are all possible collocations.

Teaching implications

Since there are no 'rules' of collocation, this aspect of vocabulary learning is often dealt with on an *ad hoc* basis; it is difficult to group items by their collocational properties, so teachers and learners are generally

	woman	man	child	dog	bird	flower	weather	landscape view	day	village house	furniture bed	picture	dress	present voice	proposal
beautiful	+	+	+	+	+	+	+	+	+	+	+	+	+	+	
lovely	+	+	(+)		+	+		+	+	+	(+)	+	+	+	
pretty	+	+	+	+	+	+		+							
charming	+	+						+	+	+	+	+		+	
attractive	+	+						+		+		+		+	+
good-looking	+	+	(+)												
handsome	+	+											+		

In speech, **beautiful**, **lovely**, **charming** and **attractive** are often used for situations in which their real meaning would be too strong, in order to express enthusiasm.

EXAMPLES

The walls were covered with a most $\left.\begin{array}{l}\textbf{beautiful}\\\textbf{lovely}\\\textbf{charming}\\\textbf{attractive}\end{array}\right\}$ wall paper.

I'll come to see you about seven – will you be there? **Beautiful** – okay – see you later.
She does really **lovely** things for people like bringing them their favourite flowers on their birthday.
Bacon and eggs for breakfast! **Lovely!**

more successful when they deal with common collocational problems in isolation or as they arise. Nevertheless, collocation can provide a useful framework for revising items which are partially known and for expanding the learner's knowledge of them. Students at intermediate level commonly use the adjectives 'light', 'weak', 'strong', 'heavy' and possibly 'mild', although they very often use them inaccurately (e.g. 'light' coffee, where 'weak' or 'mild' was intended). The following testing activity can be used to highlight the collocations while at the same time revising the adjectives.

STUDENT ACTIVITY

Look at the circles below. Do you know which adjectives you can use with the nouns in the boxes? Cross out the ones which you think are not correct:

e.g.

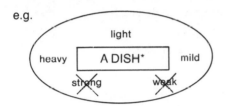

* in the sense of a plateful of cooked food e.g. 'Paella is a Spanish dish.'

Now do the same:

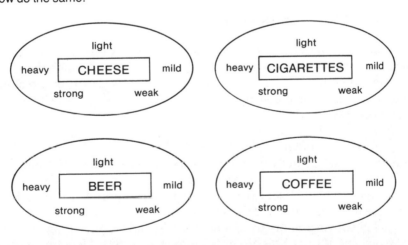

After this, students can work in pairs and ask each other what kind of cigarettes, beer, cheese and coffee they prefer.

By using this type of collocation exercise in class, teachers will be sensitising learners to the general difficulties involved and this may help them to understand the principle in future. We need to be ready to teach the types of collocation with which the learners have the greatest difficulties; those which are a source of L1 interference, for instance, and those which have restricted collocations for the average learner e.g. to spend, to waste. An item such as 'to do' has an extremely wide range of collocations and it is therefore essential to limit the examples to those which are of most benefit to the learner.

READER ACTIVITY

Look at the following list of collocations of the verb 'to do'. Decide which would be useful to teach for *productive* use to:
- a) elementary/lower-intermediate students
- b) upper-intermediate students
- c) advanced/post Cambridge First Certificate students.

to do the cooking	to do right/wrong
to do the housework	to do homework/an exercise
to do business	to do somebody a favour
to do your duty	to do somebody harm/good
to do your hair	to do somebody the honour of ...
to do somebody an injustice	to do well/badly

2.8 Componential analysis

Componential analysis is a systematic means of examining sense relations. If we take items from the same semantic field (and which therefore have some features in common with each other) we can, by breaking them down into their constituent parts, examine the similarities and differences between them.

e.g. boy = + human + male + child
      girl = + human − male + child

It is an area of semantics which is of interest and relevance to the language teacher as it represents an approach to the description of meaning of lexical items which differs from the dictionary approach. There have been recent moves to use this type of analysis to present meaning in the teaching of vocabulary to advanced levels, and we include an example here from *The Words You Need* (Rudska et al, 1981). Here, the writers have tabulated the conceptual information about the lexical items.

The grid aims to bring into focus the features which distinguish one item from another, and shows in detail how items are not truly synonymous. The principle involved here is of interest to teachers and may well allow us to aim for a more precise definition of meaning. However,

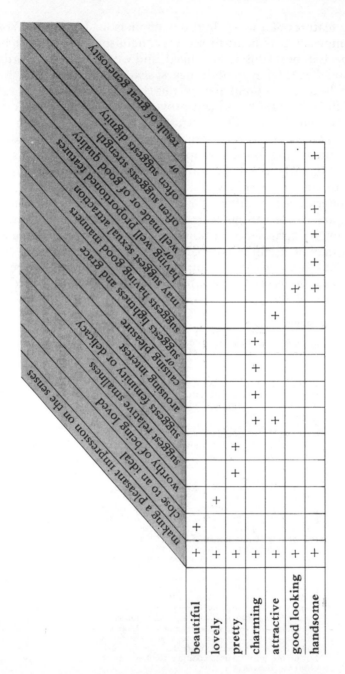

	beautiful	lovely	pretty	charming	attractive	good looking	handsome
or result of great generosity							+
often suggests strength							+
well made or of good quality							+
having well proportioned feature						+	+
may suggest sexual attraction					+		
suggest having good manners				+			
suggests lightness and grace				+			
arousing interest or causing pleasure				+	+		
suggests femininity or delicacy			+				
suggest relative smallness			+				
worthy of being loved		+					
close to an ideal	+						
making a pleasant impression on the senses	+	+	+	+	+	+	+

the idea that a word can be subjected to this type of clinical, accurate analysis is rather misleading; Leech (1983) suggests that words have 'fuzzy' meaning and that there is room for disagreement over the precise defining features of a word. In the example from *The Words You Need*, for example, it is difficult to see why 'handsome' could not be 'close to an ideal' if 'beautiful' is so defined, and we feel that the words 'handsome' and 'beautiful' may both suggest sexual attraction.

From the teacher's point of view, this type of analysis may be extremely helpful for preparation and can provide him with a framework which will allow him to consider contrasts of meaning. Although this type of study may well be appropriate for very advanced learners, our experience of attempting to use this approach with lower levels has not been successful. Clearly, the scope and complexity involved is extraordinarily difficult to limit for lower levels.

Dictionaries take a different view of the definition of meaning, and lexicographers use various techniques for illustrating meaning such as synonymy, paraphrase, or at times quite lengthy encyclopedic explanations. It may be useful to compare the treatment of the items from *The Words You Need* with some of the same items as they appear in the *Longman Dictionary of Contemporary English (LDCE)*. Notice particularly the cross-referencing:

beau·ti·ful /'bjuːtɪ̰fəl/ *adj* **1** having beauty —compare HANDSOME, PRETTY **2** *infml* very good: *a beautiful game|Your soup was really beautiful, Maude!* —**ly** *adv*

hand·some /'hænsəm/ *adj* [Wa2] **1 a** (esp. of men) good-looking; of attractive appearance: **b** (esp. of women) strong-looking; attractive with a firm, large appearance rather than a delicate one **2** generous; plentiful **3** *AmE* clever; skilful **4 handsome is as handsome does** the people who really deserve respect are those whose actions are kind or generous —**ly** *adv*

pret·ty¹ /'prɪti/ *adj* **1** [Wa1;B] (esp. of a woman, a child, or a small fine thing) pleasing or nice to look at, listen to, etc.; charming but not beautiful or grand: *She looks much prettier with long hair than with short hair.|What a pretty little garden!* —compare BEAUTIFUL, HANDSOME **2** [Wa1;B] *derog* (of a boy) charming and graceful but rather girlish **3** [Wa1;B] *apprec* (esp. of an action) causing admiration for neatness, cleverness, or skill: *He writes with a pretty turn of phrase* (=expresses himself in a delightful way) **4** [Wa5;A] *derog* not nice; displeasing: *It's a pretty state of affairs when I come home from work and you haven't even cooked my dinner!* **5** [Wa5;A] *infml* (of an amount of money) quite large: *He made a pretty fortune by selling all his land for building* —see also **a pretty** PASS³, **a pretty** PENNY (5) **6 sitting pretty** (of a person) in a favourable position or condition (without much effort) —**-tiness** *n* [U]

The Longman Lexicon of Contemporary English marries the two approaches by providing well-exemplified definitions and by grouping together items within the same semantic field, which in practical terms makes contrast more convenient:

e.g. **F39** *adjectives* : **good to look at** [B]

---

good-looking (of people) pleasant to look at: *He's a good-looking man, isn't he? She's a ʒood-looking girl too. They make a good-looking pair/couple* [⇒ C77].

beautiful 1 (usu of women, places, and things) very good-looking or worth looking at: *What a beautiful girl she is, with such beautiful long hair. This is one of the most beautiful houses in the town.* **2** *infml* very good: *That was a beautiful game of tennis.*

lovely [Wa1] **1** pleasingly beautiful: *That's a lovely dress, isn't it? What a lovely smile she has. It's a really lovely day for a picnic.* **2** *infml* very good: *It's lovely to see you again! A present for me; how lovely!* **-liness** [U]

pretty [Wa1] **1** (esp of a woman, a child, or a small thing) pleasing or nice to look at, listen to, etc; charming but not beautiful or grand: *She looks much prettier with long hair than with short hair. She has quite a pretty singing voice. What a pretty little garden.* **2** *deprec* (of a boy) charming and graceful in a girlish way **3** *apprec* causing admiration for neatness, cleverness, or skill: *That was a pretty shot—well played! He writes with a pretty turn of phrase* (= expresses himself well). **4** *derog ironical* not nice; displeasing: *It's a pretty state of affairs when I come home from work and she hasn't even cooked my dinner.*

attractive (usu of females, now increasingly of males) having good looks; pretty: *She's an attractive girl and he's an attractive man.* **un-** [*neg*] **-ness** [U] **-ly** [adv]

comely [Wa1] *old use & lit* beautiful: *She was a most comely young woman.*

handsome [Wa2] **1** (esp of men) good-looking; of attractive appearance: *He's a handsome lad, the handsomest/most handsome in town.* **2** (esp of women) attractive but looking grand rather than delicate or pretty: *What a handsome girl she is and what a fine character she has.*

Dictionaries inevitably have to compromise in their treatment of meaning. One common problem for the learner is that the lexis used in the definition may be just as difficult to understand as the target word he is seeking to clarify: this is true of native-speaker dictionaries as well as EFL ones.

3 Words and their forms

3.1 The grammar of vocabulary

At a very basic level of survival in a foreign language, we can satisfy many of our needs with vocabulary and a bilingual dictionary. A student at a school reception who is querying his sudden increase in fees would be intelligible if he said, 'I ask informations yesterday, you say me £200, no £250.' However, one reason for paying this money is to improve his English, and quite apart from possible problems of phonology or choice of functional exponents, the student needs some guidance on how to use vocabulary more accurately. Notice his failure to use past tense forms, choice of the verb 'say' instead of 'tell' with its consequent verb pattern problem, lack of preposition after 'ask', and the use of the unacceptable plural form 'informations'.

In chapter 1, activities 6 to 8, we gave examples of some of the types of grammatical errors which are relevant to the teaching of vocabulary. Since this is a book which is primarily about teaching vocabulary rather than grammar, we have limited our coverage here without, we hope, minimising the importance of it. The checklist below contains the type of questions it is useful for a teacher to ask himself when preparing a vocabulary lesson in order to anticipate potential grammatical errors. The list is by no means exhaustive, and we have restricted it to the type of information which one could normally expect to find in a good EFL dictionary. Grammarians, lexicographers and course book writers have all dealt with these areas very comprehensively, so we have included a short list of useful source books at the end of the book.

Teaching implications

There are two main pedagogic issues involved here; one is the highlighting of regular and irregular forms, and the second is the role of source books in allowing learners to be self-sufficient.

In the classroom, teachers need to clarify regular forms and common irregular forms for their students. In some cases, these will merit considerable attention: irregular verbs, verb patterns, countable and uncountable nouns, adjective versus adverb are common examples here. However, there is a danger of the grammar point becoming the overriding focus,

CHECKLIST

	Yes	No
Verbs		
1 Is the verb regular or irregular?		
2 If irregular, do the learners need to know the past tense/ past participle at this stage?		
3 Is the verb transitive, intransitive or bi-transitive?		
4 What construction does the verb take? Is the verb followed by the infinitive, '+ing' form, a 'that' clause, a preposition, nothing at all? If a preposition, what is it?		
5 If a multi-word verb, is it separable or not?		
Nouns		
1 Is the noun countable, uncountable or both, according to the context?		
2 Does it differ from the equivalent mother-tongue word in terms of countability or number?		
3 Is the plural form regular or irregular?		
4 Does it have any pronunciation or spelling difficulties when plural?		
5 Is the noun associated with a preposition? If so, what?		
6 Is it followed by a complement structure? (e.g. the need + infinitive, the idea of '+ing') If so, what?		
Adjectives		
1 Is the adjective generally followed by a preposition? (e.g. interested in something) If so, what?		
2 Is it followed by a complement structure? (e.g. important to do) If so, what?		
3 Are there any irregularities when the adjective is used as a comparative or superlative?		
Adverbs		
1 For adverbs of manner, is it easily distinguishable from the corresponding adjective? Does it have the same form as the adjective? (e.g. 'fast')		
2 Are there any problems in the formation of the comparative or superlative form?		
3 Does it have a characteristic position in the sentence?		

and of vocabulary being introduced simply to exemplify this point. As a result, low level learners sometimes learn items such as mouse/mice, wife/wives, bush/bushes, which are not very common in their plural form.

Clearly, grammar books are helpful for learners here and we have listed some useful ones at the end, but we would also like to stress the usefulness of the EFL dictionary as a source of information on the grammar of individual words. We strongly recommend making this source available to learners and training them in its use. We include here an exercise designed to illustrate the teaching of countable and uncountable nouns from *Use Your Dictionary* (Underhill, 1980).

Find these nouns in the dictionary and note whether they are [C], [U] or both. If they can be both, notice where (C) or (U) is given first.

e g improvement	[C], [U]	dependant	
e g importance	[U]	people	
e g horse	[C]	thought	
information		money	
cigarette		glass	
tobacco		luggage	
encouragement		furniture	
optimism		hope	
dictionary		advice	

Underline the correct form of the noun in these sentences.

e g How much (experience/experiences) have you got?
How many (chair/chairs) do we need?
There is too much (noise/noises).
We have only a little (tea/teas) left.
Several (student/students) have arrived.

3.2   Word building

There are three main forms of word building or word formation which are characteristic of English: affixation, compounding and conversion. *Affixation* is the process of adding prefixes and suffixes to the base item; in this way, items can be modified in meaning and/or changed from one part of speech to another. To the base form 'man', for instance, we can add prefixes and suffixes in the following way:

man
man + ly = manly
un + man + ly = unmanly
un + man + ly + ness = unmanliness

Sometimes the process of affixation produces changes in stress and sounds in an item:

e.g. democrat /'deməkraet/
democratic /demə'krætɪk/
democracy/dɪ'mɒkrəsɪ/

and may also cause spelling difficulties as in the example above (i.e. manly–manliness). Suffixes may indicate parts of speech and have little semantic value, as in the noun ending '+tion' e.g. discrimination, or may indicate the part of speech and have an intrinsic meaning e.g. '+less', as in 'hairless', 'childless', which signifies an adjective ending and also contains the idea of 'without'.

READER ACTIVITY

The following activity contains some 'potential' words – words which do not exist but which could conceivably become part of the language.
Look at each of the 'potential' items below and
a) decide what you think they would mean
b) give an example of a real word which helped you make the decision.
   e.g. a talkette
   Answer: It would probably mean a short talk, by analogy with lecturette,
            kitchenette.

1 a readeress	3 a gaolee	5 a doglet
2 lunocracy	4 a toolery	6 woolette

READER ACTIVITY

Which of the following prefixes would you be able to use with the words on the right? What meaning can you assign to each of the prefixes?

pre+ sub+	war	conservative
	modern	human
ultra+ ex+	revolutionary	

Compounding is the formation of words from two or more separate words which can stand independently in other circumstances. There are three different types of compound: adjective compounds (e.g. hard-working, time-consuming, short-sleeved, Anglo-French), verb compounds (e.g. to babysit, to sightsee), and noun compounds. For this last group, there are three main patterns: base noun + noun (e.g. a coffee jar, table tennis, horse race); possessive noun + noun (e.g. my girlfriend's brother) and prepositional structures (e.g. a look of fear, the end of the line).

Conversion, also known as zero affixation, is the process by which an item may be used in different parts of speech, yet does not change its form:

e.g. We've just had a lovely *swim*. (noun)

I can't *swim* very well. (verb)

This process is similar to suffixation in that syntactic and semantic changes may be involved, the difference being that no prefixes or suffixes are used. With certain examples of conversion, there may be phonological changes:

e.g. He works in the '*export* market.

We ex'*port* a lot of goods.

Other examples of shifting stress are 'conduct', 'conflict', 'import', 'insult', 'record', 'rebel', etc. Some may also involve sound and spelling changes:

e.g. to advise /z/ some advice /s/

Teaching implications

Focus on word building is likely to pay dividends for the learner both receptively and productively. With the receptive skills, an understanding of all three aspects of word building is essential if the learner is to make informed guesses about the meaning of unknown items. (Remember, for instance, how in the first Reader Activity in this section, you were able to deduce the meaning of items because of your understanding of suffixes.) In terms of productive skills, a knowledge of some basic principles of word building and specific examples will serve to widen a learner's range of expression.

In the classroom, the amount of time devoted to affixation and the emphasis placed on it will vary considerably according to the teaching situation. For speakers of Romance languages, certain prefixes and suffixes in English will be similar to those of the mother tongue and will cause little difficulty in terms of meaning. To dwell on the meaning of the prefix 'anti+', for example, would be as much an exercise in the knowledge of the mother tongue as in English. This does not imply that affixes similar to L1 should not be discussed; it is essential for the learner to know where similarities exist. The main priority, however, for speakers of Romance languages is phonological; these learners often have considerable difficulty in pronouncing and stressing derivatives accurately. It is also true that while many affixes are similar, there are some which would be unfamiliar e.g. '+ship', as in 'friendship', 'hardship', 'censorship', is a fairly productive suffix which does not have a direct equivalent in Latin-based languages, and would thus merit attention. The similarities or dissimilarities of English with the learner's mother tongue will determine the amount of time which needs to be spent on this area.

While it may be feasible to teach your students some generative rules concerning the formation of words with affixes, there are far fewer practical rules of compounding and conversion. For lower level students therefore, the best policy is simply to treat the derivatives as individual items and teach those which are most important for their productive (or receptive) vocabulary.

However, you may wish to deal with certain areas grammatically. A good example here would be the constructions used in noun phrases (e.g. 'the leg of the table' and 'the table leg' are acceptable, but 'the table's leg' is incorrect). A full analysis of this can be found in Swan (1980). Attention to noun + noun combinations is also helpful; students whose L1 puts modifiers after nouns tend to confuse items such as 'horse race' (i.e. a race for horses) and 'racehorse' (a horse which races). In cases such as these, the second noun generally acts as the 'head' and the first noun is used adjectivally. Where the rules of all forms of word building are too complex for the level of your students, you simply need to assess the value of teaching the derivatives of individual items. In the case of 'industry' for instance, the basic derivatives are 'industrial', 'industrialist' and 'to industrialise'. At elementary level, the last two of these are probably less useful items. (Obviously with the example above, time will need to be spent on pronunciation.)

Equally important is the need to anticipate error. In the example below many students in our experience would say 'She's a good cooker' (+er being a common prefix denoting 'agent'). Dealing with the derivatives below will also provide students with a wider range of utterances and allow them greater flexibility in production:

e.g. She	is a good cook.		
	cooks very well.	The chicken	was undercooked.
			wasn't cooked enough.
	is good at	cooking.	
		cookery.	The chicken	was overcooked.
			was cooked too long.

3.3 Pronunciation

Sadly it is not uncommon for learners of a foreign language to find that their lexical knowledge is rendered almost useless by their inability to make themselves intelligible when they speak. Such painful experiences are not confined to production either, for it is equally true that unfamiliarity with correct pronunciation can result in the learner failing to understand words in connected speech that he understands clearly in written English. Careful attention to pronunciation is therefore an essential part of vocabulary teaching if new lexis is to be used effectively, or understood without difficulty, in spoken English.

SOUNDS AND SPELLING

To many students the complex relationship between sound and spelling in English seems nothing short of a conspiracy to make the language inexplicable to foreign learners. It is easy to sympathise with this view when one considers the number of homophones in English e.g. key/quay, draft/draught; and the number of similar forms which differ widely in their pronunciation e.g. foot, flood, food. Difficult though this may be – and there are many more examples to trouble the foreign learner – it should not deter teachers from seeking out regularities which will give the learner both confidence and some measure of autonomy in tackling the pronunciation of new vocabulary. At low levels, for example, students can be made aware that the letter 'r' is silent when preceding a consonant e.g. card, park, or when it occurs at the end of a word e.g. mother, weather. The exception to this rule is when the next word begins with a vowel in which case it is usually pronounced to link the words together e.g. mother and son. Students can also be shown how the addition of an 'e' to many single syllable words ending in a vowel and consonant, transforms the vowel sound into a diphthong:

  bit/bɪt/   bite/baɪt/
  rob/rɒb/   robe/rəʊb/
  tap/tæp/   tape/teɪp/

The incidence of silent letters in pronunciation is also something that students can learn to predict from spelling patterns e.g. the silent 'k' in words beginning with 'kn' such as 'knee' or 'knife'; or the silent 'b' at the end of words preceded by an 'm' such as 'dumb' and 'bomb'. A fuller list of the rules concerning silent letters can be found in Swan (1980).

    Alongside the formulation of fairly specific rules for English pronunciation you can also provide your students with certain general guidelines that will assist them in predicting the pronunciation of new lexis. There are letters and spelling patterns which usually conform to a particular pronunciation e.g. 'au' /ɔː/, or 'igh' /aɪ/. These should be pointed out to the students wherever possible, not only for the obvious help it gives with pronunciation but also for the reassurance it provides in creating some order out of the apparent chaos.

For all the above remarks, though, it has to be admitted that the lack of consistency between spelling and pronunciation makes it exceedingly difficult if not impossible to base pronunciation on the written form. For this reason we believe that a rudimentary knowledge of phonemic symbols can greatly assist the learner by providing access to the pronunciation of new words i.e. through a dictionary, without the constant need of a teacher as intermediary. A knowledge of phonemics does not in itself mean that the learner will be able to produce accurate sounds, but the guidance it provides should enable him to approximate the sounds to a point where he is at least intelligible.

STRESS

One of the major difficulties with English pronunciation is that the position of the primary stress has such an influence on the individual vowels within a word. Thus the shift in stress from 'economist' /ɪˈkɒnəmɪst/ to 'economics' /iːkəˈnɒmɪks/ or /ekəˈnɒmɪks/ produces a different vowel quality in the first, second and third syllables. It is often this influence on surrounding syllables that makes correct stress such an important factor in being intelligible e.g. students who stress the first syllable on 'police'/pəˈliːs/ and end up producing /ˈpɒlɪs/ may find that they are not understood at all.

As with sound-spelling patterns, though, there are stress patterns which are sufficiently generative for the teacher to present as rules e.g. words with the following endings usually have the primary stress on the syllable preceding them:

+tion, +sion   education, confusion
+ic, +ical   enthusiastic, geographical
+ian   Indian, Italian

A fuller list can be found in Tench (1981).

Students can also be alerted to the regularity with which derivatives often conform to a particular shifting stress pattern e.g. verbs with three syllables or more, and ending in '+ate' usually have the main stress on the third syllable from the end and then take the '+ation' noun forming suffix to produce the following shift in stress:

cultivate	cultivation	consolidate	consolidation
dedicate	dedication	negotiate	negotiation
educate	education		

A fuller list of these shifting stress patterns can be found in Gimson and Ramsaran (1982).

Teaching implications

The degree of attention paid to the pronunciation of a lexical item will depend on the importance of the item in spoken English and the extent to which it poses problems for the students in question. For most nationalities the pronunciation of 'disaster' does not involve sound and stress difficulties that would seriously hinder intelligibility, whereas 'catastrophe' /kə'tæstrəfɪ/ would require attention to combat the natural tendency of many learners to say /'kætæstrɒf/ which would probably be understood in context but would stretch the tolerance of the listener. With items rarely used in spoken English e.g. 'henceforth', there may be a case for ignoring the pronunciation altogether. Few items, however, fall into this category so when new lexis is taught and written on the blackboard it is helpful to indicate the primary accent (assuming the item has more than one syllable) and follow the written form with a phonemic transcription if the students have previously been taught phonemics. One of the advantages of having a phonemic transcription on the board is that it acts as a reminder to the students not to be misled by the orthographic form. This can produce considerable mother-tongue interference, a very common example being the tendency of some students to revert back to strong forms for all written vowels, when in fact, their normal spoken English demonstrates an ability to produce weak forms quite naturally. If the students are used to using a particular dictionary in class it is also sensible to adopt the same symbols for marking accent, although the use of a box over the stressed symbol is easier to see e.g. alōne, as are circles denoting the number of syllables with a larger circle to indicate the main stress e.g. catastrophe oOoo. In either case we would recommend the use of different coloured chalk or boardmarkers to indicate both stress and phonemic symbols.

A further point in favour of phonemics and stress markers is that they provide valuable visual assistance. Not all language learners are blessed with a good ear for languages and can imitate or discriminate between English sounds orally from the model provided by their teacher or peer learners. For some students it is easier to grasp both sounds and stress patterns by seeing them represented graphically.

In spite of our own enthusiasm there will still be readers who are reluctant to tackle phonemics in the classroom and in some cases their fears will be quite valid. Phonemics can appear daunting and academic to some students, and if the effect of forcing phonemics upon the students is a drop in interest or motivation then it is clearly counterproductive. In our experience these fears are more apparent than real. Students derive a lot of fun and satisfaction from using phonemics and it can be incorporated into many different types of lesson in a very gentle and non-intimidating manner. The exercise below can be used to develop and consolidate several sound symbol relationships by revising irregular past tenses.

Write the past tense of the verbs below and put them into the columns below according to the pronunciation.

drive   see   bring   read   write   keep   leave   speak   choose   sleep   wear   catch

/əʊ/	/ɔː/	/e/
e.g. spoke	e.g. saw	e.g. slept

© 1986 Cambridge University Press

Practice in word stress can easily be linked to word building activities as in the exercise below.

Use a dictionary to complete the table below and mark the primary stress in each case.

Subject	Person
psychology	
history	
	engineer
economics	
politics	
	mathematician

© 1986 Cambridge University Press

An interesting way of revising this lexical set is to give the students the stress patterns and ask them to supply the right words. Thus:

Subject	Person
ooOo	oOoo
Oo	oOoo
ooOo	oooOo
oOoo	oOoo
ooOo	ooO
Ooo	ooOo

4   Decisions about content

In this chapter we are going to examine the factors which influence the teacher's selection and organisation of lexical items for the classroom, and also the role that the learner can and does play in making some of those decisions. But before considering the criteria governing how we select vocabulary, we should first say something about what we select from: how does vocabulary reach the classroom? We can identify four main sources:

1 Through the course book. This will include the written and spoken texts, activities for the presentation and practice of grammatical structures, testing exercises, and so on. Even the instructions for classroom activities can form a source of new vocabulary.
2 Through supplementary materials (not designed specifically for vocabulary development) provided by the educational institution or selected by the teacher himself. This may include texts, drills, narratives, role plays, exercises, video, etc.
3 Through the students. A wide range of unanticipated and unpredictable items will inevitably surface from student enquiries, queries, and errors.
4 Through specific vocabulary activities designed by the teacher for his particular group of students. (Along the lines of activities included in part C.)

One obvious comment on the above is that the teacher can only exercise strict control over one of the channels i.e. the fourth, through which vocabulary enters the classroom. For the rest, he can only exercise his judgement in whether to make an issue of an item once it appears. (Wherever possible, of course, these decisions should be made prior to the lesson rather than during the lesson.) If this is the case, that teachers have to contend with a wide range of miscellaneous lexis beyond their control, it is even more important that they should take very firm decisions regarding the emphasis given to individual items.

4.1   Student responsibility and teacher responsibility

In the very early stages of learning most students recognise the value of a common core of lexis that will be essential, and clearly in all their interests to learn. Once this basic level of survival has been achieved, though, lexical selection and emphasis is prone to conflicts of interest that are seldom true of grammar. For with few exceptions, most learners perceive the relevance of grammatical structures whatever their field of interest and reasons for learning the language; how it is presented is a different issue. The same cannot be said of vocabulary which is much more context-specific; items that are essential to an understanding of one field of interest may be quite irrelevant to students who are not interested in that particular subject. For this reason teachers often find it difficult to justify time being spent on lexical items that cannot command mass appeal; this leaves them with the unenviable task of constantly seeking the middle ground to satisfy disparate needs or just sustain student interest. It is a compromise that students acknowledge and generally accept, but it is a taxing situation for the teacher and far from ideal for the students.

One solution to this problem is to accept that students have different needs, and to further accept that they must assume some of the responsibility for defining those needs and the vocabulary that will be relevant to those needs. In other words, allow the students more autonomy in lexical decision-making. There are drawbacks, as the following example illustrates, but for classroom material with no obvious lexical objectives it can be a very sensible approach.

In the following text (if you are alarmed at the choice of subject matter please note that it appeared on 1 April 1984) suitable for an upper-intermediate group of students, one might select the following items as being unknown or only partially known:

to prevent	to beam
aware (of)	worship
to moor	outlaw
insatiable	clampdown
to launch	jail
to land (somebody in trouble)	

In terms of frequency, 'prevent' and 'aware' are probably the most useful items to teach, but certain students will probably know these already and may therefore wish to focus on different items. What should they choose? Nothing in the above list stands out as meriting special attention, so the teacher could be forgiven for either making an arbitrary selection or deciding that the text did not warrant any further attention to lexis. Unfortunately some students may interpret the first course of action as a waste of time and the second course of action as a denial of their right to learn. A third course of action would be to supply the students with dictionaries (they should first know how to use them), set them a time limit, and allow them to concentrate on any words they wish to learn. The teacher, meanwhile, can focus on 'prevent' and 'aware'

'Channel Sex' shock for Mrs Whitehouse

by PENDENNIS

CONFIDENTIAL documents in the possession of *The Observer* reveal a secret plan for a controversial sex film channel on British television.

Both hard core and soft porn sex films will be shown, as well as outlawed video 'nasties.'

A test transmission is scheduled for today between 10 am and noon at the time of ITV's 'Morning Worship.' It can be picked up with some fine-tuning adjustments on Channel 6 of most standard television sets.

Mrs Mary Whitehouse, chairman of the National Viewers and Listeners' Association, said yesterday that 'Channel 6 is going to show material that would land the BBC and ITV in jail.'

The controversial project, code-named 'Channel Sex,' is being run by a company registered in Panama – Alien Porn SA. The films, including 'Driller Killer' and 'I Spit on Your Grave' are to be beamed to Britain today from a specially converted boat moored in the North Sea, outside British legal jurisdiction.

If the initial reaction is favourable, Channel 6 will carry sex advertisements to finance the operation.

The Home Office is aware of today's broadcast but is powerless to prevent it. Britain is a member of the European Broadcasting Union, whose regulations prohibit the jamming of television signals within the EBU member states.

The Observer's documents show that the 'Channel Sex' project was meant to be launched next year but has been brought forward to meet 'the insatiable demand for sex and violence in Britain,' because of the clampdown on video shops.

(from *The Observer*)

for those students who do not know the items, and then monitor the other students, offering help and guidance where necessary.

Some readers may feel this is an anarchic approach to teaching, that there is no clear check on student understanding, and that their students are likely to accumulate pages of useless vocabulary; in other words an abdication of responsibility. These criticisms do have some validity, but weighed against them are two important advantages to the approach. Firstly, there is the motivation derived from learning what one wants to learn; and secondly, allowing the students to have the responsibility for making decisions (with the teacher's guidance) may well help to engender greater discrimination on their part to recognise what is useful.

The extent to which one adopts the above approach will depend on the type of students you have and the homogeneity of the group in terms of lexical needs. We have certainly found it both useful and instructive in our own classroom teaching and we thought it relevant to note some of the comments and decisions that have been made by past students with reference to the above text.

'"Prevent" is very useful – it must be because I already know it.'
'"Aware" – I didn't know this word but it looks useful.'
'"Gaol/jail" – I know the word "prison", so "gaol" isn't necessary.'
  (We pointed out that 'gaol' might be useful receptively for this level of student as it appears frequently in newspaper texts.)
'"Beam" – it's a technological word so it may become more important in the future; that's why I chose to learn it.'
  (We pointed out that for a banker with no specific interest in technology, this item probably wasn't very useful.)
'"Launch" – I think this is useful because my other teacher taught it to us last week.'
'"Launch" – this word will be useful because I work in marketing.'
'I want to learn them all. I think they're all useful.'
  (We suggested to this student that her approach might interfere with the learning of more useful items.)
'"Moor" – I'm very interested in boats so this word will be useful.'
Student: 'Moor' – is this word only used for boats?
Teacher: Yes.
Student: In that case I don't want to learn it.

This type of activity can be very revealing for the teacher as a means of understanding his students' needs and attitudes towards learning. Clearly the student must be involved in the decisions about items to be learnt, but from the comments above it is equally clear that the students need guidance and that the teacher must not only strive to discover their needs but must also assume some responsibility for selection.

4.2 Criteria for selection

It is stating the obvious to say that the selected lexical items should be useful, but how do we determine exactly what is useful? In the first place we have to concede that every teaching situation is different and so essential items in one context may be quite useless in another. The relative importance you attach to the various criteria described below will therefore depend on your own teaching situation.

4.2.1 FREQUENCY

The high frequency of an item is no guarantee of usefulness, but there is obviously a significant correlation between the two so it is worth examining some of the work on frequency word-counts that has been carried out over recent decades.

One of the most widely known word-counts is the *General Service List of English Words* (compiled and edited by Dr Michael West, 1953). Its aim was to scientifically select and compile the 2,000 most commonly used words in English from a study of 5 million (or for some words $2\frac{1}{2}$ million) running words of written English. The list also took account of the frequency of different semantic values within those words possessing more than one meaning; for this reason there are closer to 6,000 entries in the *General Service List*, although the number of headwords is, as stated, only 2,000.

Since the publication of the *General Service List* there have been a number of published frequency counts. The Kucera and Francis list (1967) enlisted the aid of computers in compiling an initial list of 2,000 words, later expanded to 5,000 words, and the *Threshold Level* (1975) prepared for the Council of Europe by J. van Ek includes a lexicon of approximately 1,500 items. The *Threshold Level* attempted to define a minimum level of 'general ability' and the authors suggest that two-thirds of the lexicon would be required for productive use.

A third, and easily available word-count is the *Cambridge English Lexicon* (compiled by Roland Hindmarsh, 1980). Hindmarsh set out to define a comprehension lexicon (i.e. receptive vocabulary) that would be sufficient for students to pass the Cambridge First Certificate Examination. The result is a list of 4,500 words with over 8,000 semantic values. One feature of this list that makes it particularly relevant for course designers is that the items have been graded on a frequency scale 1–5, thus providing an approximate guide as to when items should be introduced on a course leading to Cambridge First Certificate. An additional scale 6–7 is used for the less frequent semantic values of a word; these values are likely to be more relevant to students studying for the Cambridge Proficiency Examination.

The contents of frequency counts should not be accepted uncritically or used dogmatically to dictate lexical grading. Their value must be judged against the source of the data and criteria governing inclusion of the data, as this may greatly affect their relevance to your students. For example, the bias towards the written word upon which frequency counts are based may obviously conflict with the usefulness of items in spoken English. And even if we accept the legitimacy of the items included, there will still be occasions when usefulness is not determined by frequency. An item of low frequency may be vital if it is the only word that expresses a particular semantic value and cannot be paraphrased easily. We have found, both as teachers and learners, that an 'adaptor' for electrical appliances is a very useful item when travelling in a foreign country but it is not an item of vocabulary that appears in many word-counts or low level course books. It exemplifies the type of item that has a high frequency in certain situations although the overall frequency may be very low. The converse of this situation is where knowledge of one particular item will satisfactorily cover the meaning of other items and so render them redundant. For receptive purposes it may be useful to know 'sweater', 'jumper' and 'pullover', but for productive purposes one of those words should be sufficient.

4.2.2   CULTURAL FACTORS

One drawback of word-counts we have not mentioned is, that being based on the utterances of native speakers they will obviously reflect the cultural interests of these speakers. Such interests may not, however, be shared by L1 learners, who may wish to express ideas and experiences quite outside those of a native speaker. Landscape and environment are examples of this; 'sleet' and 'double-glazing' as lexical items are about as useful to Brazilians as 'mangos' and 'cockroaches' are to Scandinavians (while they remain in their home environment). And at a socio-cultural level there are topics that take on a significance in certain countries which is far in excess of their importance to the majority of British English or American English speakers e.g. 'referenda' in Switzerland or 'catholicism' in Spain and Italy. Inappropriate lexical selection is just one of the pitfalls of cultural ethnocentricity, and for native speakers working abroad this area may warrant considerable attention; not only in terms of vocabulary but of the whole syllabus.

4.2.3   NEED AND LEVEL

Common sense dictates that students who are required to read technical reports in English in their native country will have different lexical needs to those learners who want survival English for travel purposes in English-speaking countries. Equally obvious is that elementary students will recognise limitations in their selection of lexis that will not be true of advanced learners. Conflict arises, though, when the lexical needs of the learner would seem to be incongruous with his general language level. This is a potential problem for course book writers designing Business English or Technical English material for low level students. How does one reconcile the need for highly technical vocabulary alongside the apparent inability of the students to manage very basic grammatical structures? There is no easy answer to this problem, although we believe current practice frequently errs on the side of asserting the supremacy of level over need. The crucial issue here is one of motivation. If the student does not perceive the vocabulary input to be useful it will be difficult to engage his interest and so effective learning of everything else will also be reduced. It is not therefore the question of lexical supremacy over grammar but that relevant lexical input is likely to contribute to the effectiveness of the overall programme.

READER ACTIVITY

1 The items below have been taken from a page of the *Cambridge English Lexicon*, except that we have omitted the frequency scale 1–7 that Hindmarsh includes. Assuming that 1 represents beginners/post beginners, 5 represents Cambridge First Certificate (low advanced) and 7 Cambridge Proficiency (very advanced), what grade would you attach to each of the items? If your answers differ widely from the *Lexicon* you might consider the factors, other than frequency, that influenced your choice.

devil
  n. Satan, any evil spirit, a bad man
  n. term of pity: *queer devil; poor devil*
diagram *n.*
dial
  v. telephone: *I've dialled them three times*
  n. face of a measuring device: *the dial on a radio*
diameter *n.*
diamond
  n. precious stone
  n. shaped in parallelogram: *diamond-pattern quilt*
diary *n.*
dictate *v.* speak for recording: *dictate to a secretary*
dictation *n.* passage that is dictated, activity of dictating

dictionary *n.*
die
  v. decease
  v. become weak: *interest in it died*
  v. long: *dying for a drink*
differ
  v. be unlike: *they differ in their tastes*
  v. not agree: *I differ from you about that*
difference
  n. unlikeness: *there's a big difference in attitude*
  n. gap: *there's a difference of nearly a kilo*
different
  adj. unlike: *this pencil is different from mine*
  adj. other: *this is a different way we are taking*

2 The pairs of words below provide semantic cover for each other. If you had to choose one item to teach from each pair what would it be?

sociable	gregarious
to tremble	to shake
seat	bench
lately	recently

3 Look at the picture and then consider the questions below.

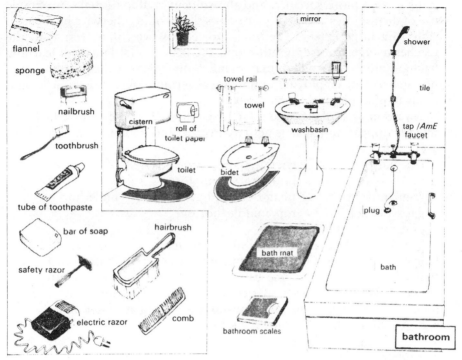

(from *Longman Dictionary of Contemporary English*)

Which items would you teach to:
a) Beginner/elementary students studying in an English-speaking country?
b) Beginner/elementary students studying in a country where English is not the native language?
c) Intermediate students in an English-speaking country?
d) Intermediate students in any other country?
Of items still to be taught (if any), are there any items that you consider are not worth teaching even to advanced students? Would you change them for any other items?

4.2.4 EXPEDIENCY

The classroom will often dictate the need for certain vocabulary, without which the students may fail to understand their teacher, fellow students or the activity they are supposedly engaged in. One such area is grammatical terminology, and although many teachers are loath to burden their students with too many grammatical labels, a shared understanding of

61

certain items can be an asset. Highlighting is often made easier, explanations can be more succinct, and the student is able to make profitable use of dictionaries and grammar books that would otherwise be inaccessible to a large extent. The final choice, however, must rest with the teacher as age, course duration and the educational language learning background of the students may significantly influence the possible benefits or harm of employing grammatical terminology. The same would apply to phonological terminology.

A second area of classroom language includes those items which frequently appear in language activity instructions. Common among these are:

true/false	get into pairs / groups
tick/cross	grid/chart/map/form
regular/irregular	fill in / cross out / leave out / underline
gaps/blanks	top/middle/bottom
offer/accept/refuse/invite	
instruction/description/suggestion/opinion	

Constant exposure alone usually guarantees that these items will eventually be absorbed, but one can hasten the process in a positive way by designing classroom activities that will incorporate many of these items and so avoid confusion or misunderstanding at a later date.

e.g. Ask the students to study the following:

STUDENT ACTIVITY

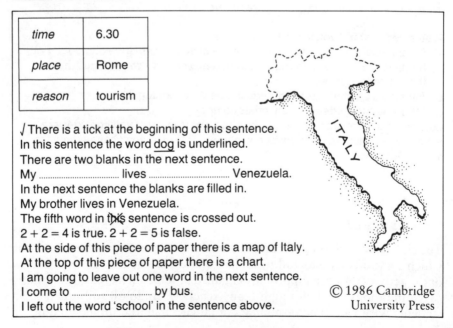

time	6.30
place	Rome
reason	tourism

√ There is a tick at the beginning of this sentence.
In this sentence the word <u>dog</u> is underlined.
There are two blanks in the next sentence.
My .... lives .... Venezuela.
In the next sentence the blanks are filled in.
My brother lives in Venezuela.
The fifth word in this sentence is crossed out.
2 + 2 = 4 is true. 2 + 2 = 5 is false.
At the side of this piece of paper there is a map of Italy.
At the top of this piece of paper there is a chart.
I am going to leave out one word in the next sentence.
I come to .... by bus.
I left out the word 'school' in the sentence above.

© 1986 Cambridge
University Press

The following items could then be elicited and written on the blackboard:

to put a | tick / cross	top/bottom
to leave out something	true/false
to underline something	a map/chart
to cross out something	a blank
to fill in something e.g. to fill in a blank	

Now do the following exercise:

STUDENT ACTIVITY

1 Write your name above this sentence and underline it.
2 Cross out the third word in the first sentence.
3 Draw a map of your country at the top of this piece of paper.
4 Put a tick at the end of this question.
5 Leave out question 6.
6 Ask your teacher a question.
7 Write a false sentence about yourself at the bottom of the page.
8 Put a cross in the middle of your map.
9 Fill in the blanks in question 10.
10 My name is ....
11 Is the answer to question 10 true or false?
12 Get into groups and check your answers.

Then, of course, there will be vocabulary the students need in order to ask relevant questions and obtain further information. High on a beginner's list of lexical priorities will be 'repeat', 'write' and/or 'spell', 'mean', 'explain' and 'pronounce'. This will be true both inside and outside the classroom but particularly inside the classroom where there is a source i.e. the teacher, to satisfy these needs. Outside the classroom a satisfactory source may not either be available or sought so the need for the questions may not arise.

As the students' language level develops, so will their desire for more complex classroom language, in order to answer their queries and satisfy their curiosity e.g. define, analyse, imply. Although these items have been included under a label of expediency they should not be regarded as a regrettable necessity, but as a category of language that does serve a vital function and is perceived to be important by the students. Without it they will experience considerable frustration.

Expedient vocabulary teaching also occurs when:

– The classroom activity demands it e.g. items that are not intrinsically useful may be taught if they serve another function such as providing the necessary language to negotiate a role play / simulation.
– A classroom activity engages the students' interest to such an extent that it seems worthwhile to include lexis that might otherwise be deemed irrelevant e.g. the words of a song.
– The student demands to know the meaning of a word. When this happens (and it happens all the time), teachers have to use their discretion in deciding whether the question is sufficiently relevant to take up classroom time. If teachers give in to every student request for information they are likely to be distracted from the main teaching aim, and worse still, the lesson is in danger of degenerating into a 'stream of consciousness' approach to vocabulary teaching which is unlikely to be very constructive. The opposite philosophy i.e. ignore all questions and plough on with the lesson plan, is equally damaging. Students find it very frustrating and demotivating to have information withheld, particularly if they are struggling to express themselves and lack the necessary vocabulary.
– The course book dictates it.

4.3   Receptive versus productive vocabulary

To define our terms here, we understand 'receptive' vocabulary to mean language items which can only be recognised and comprehended in the context of reading and listening material, and 'productive' vocabulary to be language items which the learner can recall and use appropriately in speech and writing. (These terms are often called 'passive' and 'active' vocabulary.)

Consider your mother tongue, for instance. There will be items which you are able to recognise and understand, but which you find difficult to recall or do not know sufficiently well to use accurately. There will be other items which you understand, but do not use, perhaps because they occur in contexts or types of discourse which are alien to you. We include here an example of the second type which we feel confident we would not use except as an example in this book:

His salary is *incommensurate* with his ability.

With native speakers, receptive vocabulary far exceeds productive vocabulary; an educated speaker is able to 'understand' between 45,000 and 60,000 items, although no native speaker would pretend that his productive vocabulary would approach this figure.

In the language learning situation, we would stress the importance of decision-making by the teacher and materials writer about which items are worth learning for productive use and which are only useful for purposes of recognition. This decision-making has several implications; the teacher will need to select what he feels will be most relevant for the students' productive vocabulary and this, in turn, will affect his treatment of those items in the classroom. Clearly, the teacher has a great responsibility since his knowledge of the complexities and usefulness of the item is likely to be superior to the student's knowledge. Nevertheless, the learner may be in a much stronger position to decide whether an item is worth acquiring productively; this is particularly true in the case of ESP students. It is also worth stating at this point that the learner who perceives the vital personal relevance of an item may well acquire it whether the teacher pays great attention to it or not. Conversely, the learner may consciously or subconsciously reject items which the teacher is trying to teach him.

Very often this transition of an item from a student's receptive vocabulary to his productive one is a gradual process. Repeatedly hearing or reading the item over a period of time is often the most common way in which this transition takes place. In the classroom, teachers may at times be attempting to speed up this process by 'making an issue' of the item: that is, clarifying its meaning and form and encouraging controlled and freer practice.

Polarising vocabulary into productive and receptive categories in this way may seem rather artificial, and indeed in many cases the decisions to be made are by no means clear-cut. Nonetheless it seems useful to bear the distinction in mind and to strive towards selectivity based on the students' needs and learning environment.

Look at the following activity to exemplify the point above. Imagine that you have at your disposal a text which includes the following items of vocabulary.

a splint	dosage	plasters
a wound	to faint	to be sick (i.e. vomit)
harmful	to come to	diarrhoea
to hurt	period	

You intend to use this text with an intermediate level class of general English students in your own teaching environment. Which items do you think:
a) your students would need as part of their productive vocabulary?
b) your students would need as part of their receptive vocabulary?
c) your students would probably not need to know at all?

You will almost certainly find that there are some items which fit clearly into categories (a), (b) and (c) above, but others which are more difficult to categorise and your decision will depend very much on the individual student and his present and future needs.

With reference to the above text, imagine yourself to be in the following situations. Notice how your decisions differ. (Remember the target groups are all intermediate level.)
1 You are teaching a group of adult students who are planning a holiday in an English-speaking country.
2 You are teaching a group of fourteen to fifteen year olds who have studied English for three years in their own country and have to pass school exams.
3 You are teaching a group of nurses in their own country who frequently deal with English-speaking tourists in the Casualty Department.

4.4 How many items to teach

We need to consider two questions in this section. First, there is the optimum vocabulary load for a single sixty-minute lesson, and second, the number of items that should be covered over the duration of the course.

For the reasons listed at the end of this chapter, it is impossible to be dogmatic about the number of new lexical items that should be presented in a sixty-minute lesson. We would suggest an average of eight to twelve productive items as representing a reasonable input; the lower figure being more suitable for elementary students and the upper figure for more advanced students. If this rate of input were then sustained for the duration of the course we can calculate that low level students would achieve a productive vocabulary of approximately 1,000 items over 125 hours of study. In other words the students would possess the lexicon considered necessary to meet the level of 'general ability' defined in the *Threshold Level* (see p. 58). How realistic is this goal? Professor van Ek states that the original intention had been to establish the height of the Threshold level on the basis of 100–25 hours of study, but concedes that the aim was rather ambitious. Although there is no conclusive evidence to support this opinion we feel that most teachers would instinctively endorse the view that 1,000 items was beyond the capacity of most learners with 125 hours study. So, while it may be reasonable to present eight items per lesson, it is probably unrealistic to expect the majority of students to retain this number over the duration of the course. Highly intensive courses are likely to produce a degree of forgetting caused by 'interference', while students on courses that only provide a few hours study a week will inevitably suffer memory failure as a result of 'decay'. These two processes are discussed in detail in chapter 6.

The extent to which learners may fall short of the desired lexicon over the duration of the course, will depend on a number of factors. Students in an English-speaking country will have far greater exposure to the language and this should help them, not only in the retention of items previously encountered but also in the acquisition of new items. For learners in their own country much will depend on individual motivation, the priority given to the language course amongst their other commitments, and any contact with the language they might have outside of the classroom e.g. through books, films, work, or perhaps native speakers of English. In this context homework can play a very important role in vocabulary development. Workbooks or practice books accompanying major course books can compensate for restricted classroom time, and provide a source for lexical consolidation as well as an opportunity for learners to acquire vocabulary relevant to their own personal needs.

EXTERNAL FACTORS TO BE CONSIDERED

a) *How similar in form is the target item to an equivalent in the learner's own language?*
   Cognates such as 'taxi', 'hotel' and 'bar' should only cause phonological problems and are thus useful to deal with early on when teaching beginners; they can give the learner a sense of satisfaction as well as allowing him to focus on a new phonological system. However, items which appear to be cognates such as 'toast' (*le toast* in French) may require attention not only to pronunciation but also to syntax: 'toast' is uncountable in English but countable in French. False cognates such as 'library' (*la librairie* in French means 'bookshop') will also demand considerable conscious attention and effort on the part

of the student. Anything else which is completely removed from the learner's own language will obviously be more difficult to memorise.

b) *How easy is it to illustrate the meaning?*
Concrete items which can be represented visually or demonstrated simply (e.g. to hit, a table) can inevitably be dealt with more economically than abstract items (e.g. an experience, upset (adjective)). In monolingual teaching situations, translation is often a useful shortcut, but this resource may not be available for multilingual classes. There are also areas where there is no direct, clear translation, and as levels of sophistication increase, dealing with meaning and form becomes a time-consuming activity.

c) *What is the student's learning environment?*
Factors such as the intensiveness of the course, the time of day, whether the students are working or studying outside their language classroom will all have some bearing on the vocabulary load which they can handle.

d) *What language aptitude do the learners have?*
Learners who fail to adopt effective language learning strategies, or who have a poor memory for language items, or great difficulty with phonology, will probably be unable to absorb as many items as 'good' learners. They may need more training in learning skills. Age will also affect the number of items which can be learnt. For instance, many teachers tend to restrict the number of items when teaching young children.

e) *What else dictates the syllabus, apart from the teacher?*
Is there a school syllabus to be covered? What is the students' learning goal? For many teachers, the course book dictates the selection and number of items, and in our experience, students are often overloaded with vocabulary in their course books rather than underloaded. (See chapter 12 on vocabulary in course books.)

FACTORS WITHIN THE TEACHER'S CONTROL

a) *What else do you intend to cover within the timetable?*
If the teacher expects to deal with new structures or functional exponents in the same lesson, then the amount of new vocabulary will have to be severely curtailed.

b) *How much exposure will you give to the item?*
The amount of time and effort devoted to exposure, practice and revision are vital factors in retention and in ensuring that items become part of a student's productive vocabulary.

4.5 Grouping of items of vocabulary

Since vocabulary consists of a series of interrelating systems and is not just a random collection of items, there seems to be a clear case for presenting items to a student in a systematised manner which will both illustrate the organised nature of vocabulary and at the same time enable him to internalise the items in a coherent way.

Semantic fields, or, as they are commonly called in pedagogical terms, lexical sets, are made up of sets of semantically similar items. These fields may range from very broad categories, such as 'life and living things' to smaller areas such as 'kinds of man' (e.g. man, gentleman, fellow) or 'kinship relations' (e.g. son, daughter), and clearly the same item will occur in different fields. 'Man' may occur in a semantic field with 'types of mammal' or 'types of servant' or 'human gender'. From the teacher's point of view, too, many of the groupings listed below are convenient. Lexical sets, for example, form useful 'building blocks' and can be revised and expanded as students progress; they often provide a clear context for practice as well.

The groupings below consist of different types of semantic fields as well as phonological and grammatical sets. Clearly, some groupings are more appropriate at certain levels than at others.

Items related by topic
One of the most common and useful groupings found in course books e.g. types of fruit, articles of clothing, living room furniture, etc.

Items grouped as an activity or process (also topic-related)
For example the steps involved in starting a car, buying a house, etc. (see p. 154).

Items which are similar in meaning
These are items which are easily confused e.g. pretty, lovely, attractive.

Also to be included within this grouping are commonly taught sets such as 'ways of walking' (e.g. limp, tiptoe, amble, etc.) or 'ways of looking' (e.g. peer, squint, glance, stare, etc.).

This type of group needs to be handled extremely carefully; the items need to be contextualised properly, and it is vital to highlight to students the differences between items as clearly as possible. One common danger is that grouping items in this way may force teachers into including items of different levels of usefulness or frequency for the sake of 'neatness'.

Items which form 'pairs'
These can be synonyms, contrasts and 'opposites' e.g. old/new, buy/sell,

lend/borrow, obstinate/stubborn. Contextualisation is essential here. For detailed comments on these, consult section 2.4.

Items along a scale or cline, which illustrate differences of degree

For example describing an essay – excellent / very good / good / satisfactory /weak
human age – a child / a teenager / an adult

The meaning of items within a scale or cline is obviously relative; for example, a hot day is not the same as a hot furnace, but this rarely causes confusion in context.

Items within 'word families' i.e. derivatives

It is often possible to group items of vocabulary to illustrate the principles of word building, the meanings of prefixes and suffixes and the related phonological difficulties:

e.g. bi'ology   bi'ologist   bio'logical
psy'chology   psy'chologist   psycho'logical

or pleasant – unpleasant
helpful – unhelpful
sympathetic – unsympathetic
friendly – unfriendly

Items grouped by (a) grammatical similarity and (b) notional similarity

This can be particularly useful at lower levels when dealing with areas such as adverbs of frequency or prepositions, but may be just as relevant at later levels to group together nouns with irregular plurals, or words expressing probability or possibility (e.g. There is a good chance that …, He's likely to …, It's bound to …).

Items which connect discourse

There are a variety of different types of connectives which act as 'signposts' in discourse and can be grouped and treated as lexical items. The grouping of sentence adverbials used in listing, for example, could include 'to begin with', 'in the second place', 'last of all'. In a similar type of grouping, one might find items such as 'unless', 'otherwise', 'or else', 'provided (that)' which are related in that they impose some form of condition.

Adverbs ending in '+ly' (e.g. unfortunately, happily, surprisingly) are also important connectives, but may not cause as much difficulty as the examples above e.g. He ran out of cash. Fortunately, he had his American Express card with him.

This is an extremely important area since an understanding of these 'signposts' is vital in comprehension, and unless they are understood, contextual guesswork may become almost impossible. We have provided a classroom activity for this on page 137.

Items forming a set of idioms or multi-word verbs

Certain sets of multi-word verbs or idioms can form coherent groups e.g. to ring up, to call up, to get through, to ring back; out of sorts, under the weather, on top of the world.

However, these groupings are fairly restricted in practice and it is often easier to teach these as and when they arise (see ch. 3).

Items grouped by spelling difficulty or phonological difficulty

This can be approached within a topic area e.g. food vocabulary – menu, pie, vegetable, recipe, tough meat, steak.

Items grouped by style

This may be a useful way to distinguish between items which are neutral or colloquial: cigarette = ciggy, toilet = loo.
Similarly to deal with British and American English: petrol = gasoline, pavement = sidewalk, lorry = truck.

An item explored in terms of its different meanings

At later levels there is a need for the student to expand his knowledge of known items. He may, for instance, be aware that 'sentence' can mean a grammatical unit consisting of clauses and/or phrases, but he will need to learn that it also means a punishment given by a judge.

Items causing particular difficulty within one nationality group

This may be a useful way of highlighting the dangers of false cognates (see ch. 1, activities 1 and 2) or of dealing with the phonological difficulties common to one group. For instance, when teaching Japanese students to discriminate and be able to produce /f/, a vocabulary activity on the topic area of reacting to films, books, plays, etc. could include a selection of items containing the sound /f/ e.g. frightening, funny, fantastic, awful, fabulous.

However, there are certain features of vocabulary which defy methodology. A coherent and meaningful group of *collocations* is often difficult to organise and it may be better to teach these as they arise. Nevertheless, it is sometimes possible to group these by topic, as in the case of food items: sweet/dry wine, tough/tender meat, fresh/stale bread, etc. As mentioned elsewhere, *connotation* may also be difficult to deal with as a coherent grouping (though this may be possible with certain topic areas such as politics) and it is often best handled through text work or as it arises.

Suggested activities

1 Take a unit from the course book you are using at present with students and make a critical assessment of the selection. Have the authors made decisions for you about productive or receptive vocabulary? Is the unit overloaded or underloaded? How appropriate is this selection for your students? Is it well-organised?

2 Try an experiment with your class on similar lines to the one outlined on pages 55–7 of this unit.

3 Can you think of items which your students commonly find difficult to recall, and which like 'adaptor' (see p. 59) are difficult to express in other words?

4 What sort of items regularly appear in the course books and supplementary books you use which you feel are unsuitable for your students, for cultural or environmental reasons?

5 If you feel that the activity on pages 62–4 for teaching classroom language was useful, and you also make use of grammatical terminology in class, devise a similar sort of activity to teach or check this vocabulary. (You might make use of a series of sentences with grammatical errors, for instance.)

6 Look back at the section on grouping of items of vocabulary, and add at least one more example to each category.

5 How the learner discovers meaning

5.1 Traditional approaches and techniques used in the presentation of new vocabulary items

We will now examine the most common ways in which meaning of new items is conveyed in a normal teaching situation. Although 'traditional approaches and techniques' may sound pejorative, it is not intended to be; indeed, a teacher who was not able to make use of the following techniques might feel severely handicapped. Most of these are means which tend to be associated with a more teacher-centred approach and consequently the items taught through these means are usually selected by the teacher rather than the learner. They may be used for teaching incidental items or in a 'vocabulary lesson'.

5.1.1 VISUAL TECHNIQUES

Visuals
These include flashcards, photographs, blackboard drawings, wallcharts and realia (i.e. objects themselves). They are extensively used for conveying meaning and are particularly useful for teaching concrete items of vocabulary such as food or furniture, and certain areas of vocabulary such as places, professions, descriptions of people, actions and activities (such as sport and verbs of movement). They often lend themselves easily to practice activities involving student interaction. For example, a set of pictures illustrating sporting activities could be used as a means of presenting items such as skiing, sailing, climbing, etc. These visual aids can then be used as the basis for a guided pair work dialogue:

e.g. Have you ever been (skiing)?

Yes, I went to Italy last year. ↙   ↘ No, I haven't. Have you?
Did you enjoy it?   etc.
etc.

Mime and gesture
These are often used to supplement other ways of conveying meaning. When teaching an item such as 'to swerve', a teacher might build a

situation to illustrate it, making use of the blackboard and gesture to reinforce the concept.

5.1.2 VERBAL TECHNIQUES

1 Use of illustrative situations (oral or written)

This is most helpful when items become more abstract. To ensure that students understand, teachers often make use of more than one situation or context to check that learners have grasped the concept. To illustrate the meaning of 'I don't mind', the following context may be useful:

Ali likes *Dallas* and *Upstairs, Downstairs* equally.

Unfortunately, they are both on television at the same time. It doesn't matter to him which programme he watches. How does he answer this question?

Teacher: Do you want to watch *Dallas* or *Upstairs, Downstairs*?

Ali:　　 I...

The teacher could then follow this with a check question to ensure that the concept has been grasped: 'Does he want to watch one programme more than another?' He may then encourage students to use the idiom in different contexts, for instance: 'Do you want tea or coffee?' in order to elicit 'Tea, please,' or 'Coffee, please' or 'I don't mind'.

2 Use of synonymy and definition

Teachers often use synonymy with low level students, where inevitably they have to compromise and restrict the length and complexity of their explanations. It would, for example, be justifiable at low levels to tell students that 'miserable' meant 'very sad'. Secondly, it is commonly used with higher level students and subsequently qualified. 'Bloke', for instance, means the same as 'man', but is colloquial. This qualification is clearly very important.

Definition alone is often inadequate as a means of conveying meaning, and clearly contextualised examples are generally required to clarify the limits of the item. For example, 'to break out' in 'a fire broke out' has the sense of 'to start', but this would be a misleading definition for a learner and might encourage him to think that 'the lesson broke out' was acceptable English.

3 Contrasts and opposites

As with synonymy, this is a technique which students themselves use, often asking 'What's the opposite of...?' A new item like 'sour' is easily illustrated by contrasting it with 'sweet' which would already be known by intermediate level students. However, it is vital to illustrate the contexts in which this is true. Sugar is sweet and lemons are sour, but the opposite of sweet wine isn't sour wine, and the opposite of sweet tea isn't sour tea.

4   Scales

Once students have learnt two contrasting or related gradable items, this can be a useful way of revising and feeding in new items. If students know 'hot' and 'cold', for example, a blackboard thermometer can be a framework for feeding in 'warm' and 'cool' and later 'freezing' and 'boiling'. Similarly with adverbs of frequency:

	never	
	hardly ever	
I	occasionally	go to the cinema on Sundays.
	sometimes	
	often	
	always	

These can also be given in a jumbled version for students to put in an appropriate order.

5   Examples of the type

To illustrate the meaning of superordinates such as 'furniture', 'vegetables', 'meat' and 'transport', it is a common procedure to exemplify them e.g. table, chair, bed and sofa are all *furniture*. Some of these can of course also be dealt with through visual aids.

5.1.3   TRANSLATION

We have spoken to teachers who have admitted to feeling guilty about the use of translation in the classroom; almost as if they were cheating. This is quite ridiculous, for translation can be a very effective way of conveying meaning. It can save valuable time that might otherwise be spent on a tortuous and largely unsuccessful explanation in English, and it can be a very quick way to dispose of low frequency items that may worry the students but do not warrant significant attention. For monolingual groups it is also a valid approach to highlight the danger of false cognates: for example, the French word *sensible* would be translated as 'sensitive' in English, and not 'sensible'.

Some would argue that translation may be legitimate for items possessing a clear mother-tongue equivalent, but should otherwise be avoided. This is possibly overstating the case. Translation may not always convey the exact sense of an item, but then neither do English synonyms or definitions on many occasions. A more real danger with translation is that if students continue to use the mother tongue as a framework on which to attach L2 items, they will not develop the necessary framework to take account of sense relations between different items in the new language.

If teachers rely too heavily on the use of translation and deliver most explanations in the mother tongue, their students are surely losing some of the essential spirit and atmosphere of being in a language learning classroom. They are also being denied access to listening practice for which there is usually a high degree of interest and motivation. In our experience students rarely listen so intently than when they are learning new words. Used sensibly though, translation is far too valuable not to be exploited.

5.2 Student-centred learning

There has been a trend in recent years to develop more self-access materials, and in the classroom a desire to shift the focus away from the teacher and concentrate on more student-centred activities. This not only makes the student more responsible for his own learning but also permits greater attention to individual needs.

These developments are very relevant to vocabulary teaching. After elementary level, it becomes increasingly difficult for the teacher to select vocabulary that will be equally useful to all his students. This difficulty is compounded in the case of teachers working in an English-speaking country as their students come from different countries and learning backgrounds. Placement tests may group students in terms of lexical volume (this will be very approximate) but there will still remain significant differences in actual content. Thus time spent teaching new vocabulary may be wasted on some of the group (who already know it), even if as teachers we often justify this by calling it 'revision'. On a general English course, compromise is inevitable, and in the previous chapter we discussed the need for the teacher to take responsibility for the selection of items on the students' behalf, not only because of the teacher's greater knowledge of the language, but also because of his central role in appreciating and integrating the different needs of the class members. However, from the items the teacher provides, the learner can go on to select even more rigorously in accordance with his own knowledge and needs.

Attention to individual needs is not the only reason for encouraging different approaches to vocabulary teaching. We know from experience that unanticipated lexical items inevitably surface during the course of a lesson, and with the constant clamour for definitions and explanations it is very easy for the focus to shift back almost entirely to the teacher as he produces on-the-spot answers to these questions. Carried to extremes, this leaves the teacher very vulnerable to the criticism of dominating the lesson. If we acknowledge that such intervention on the part of the teacher is both necessary and useful, and that it will probably involve making use of traditional approaches to vocabulary teaching, there is a growing case for designing more student-centred activities for intended lexical input.

Recent developments have emphasised the importance of equipping students with the necessary strategies for dealing with skills activities. In the learning of vocabulary this involves:
1 Asking others.
2 Using a dictionary.
3 Making use of context to deduce meaning and guessing from the item itself.

We are now going to examine these strategies in more detail. In each case we will look at examples of activities which attempt to integrate the presentation of new lexis with a useful learning strategy, and allow the learner some autonomy.

5.2.1 ASKING OTHERS

A student can ask the teacher or another student to explain the meaning of an item which he has just encountered. Conversely, there are occasions when a student finds that he wants to use a particular item but does not know how to say it in English. The best strategy is for the student to make the context sufficiently clear so that the listener can then provide the student with the word he is looking for. For example, 'My hands are very cold so I want to buy some...' (The speaker would probably also use mime to clarify.) A native speaker listening to this could provide the word 'gloves'.

In addition, it would be helpful to equip the students with the expressions below, which would help them to elicit the target items:
e.g. It's where you (e.g. wash dishes).

It's when you (e.g. pass another car on the road).

It's the | thing you (e.g. use for cleaning the floor).
           | stuff

What's this called in English?

What's the opposite of (e.g. beautiful)?

We are including here a classroom activity designed to help students with this type of strategy.

Below you will find a set of pictures of household gadgets. A teacher might proceed by distributing copies of the sheet and asking students to write the names of any items they already know. At this stage, students

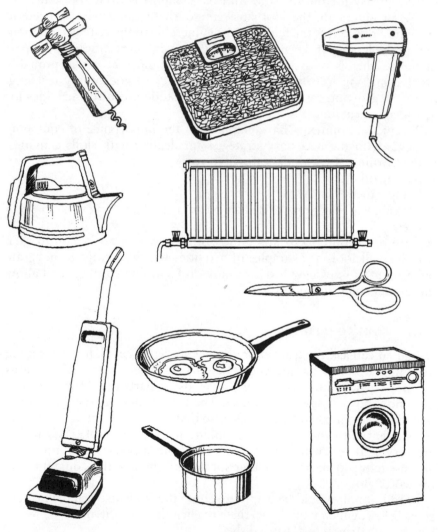

© 1986 Cambridge University Press

will be working individually. It would then be useful to teach the structure, 'What's the thing you use for (+gerund)?' to enable the students to go on to ask each other about any of the items they do not know. The teacher will need to monitor carefully to clarify meaning, check pronunciation and spelling and supply the correct answer where necessary, but otherwise the activity can be entirely student-centred. The amount of intervention by the teacher while monitoring will clearly depend on the teacher himself, the ability of the groups to work well together and the accuracy of the information exchange. The teacher may well decide to have a final feedback session with the class to ensure that the activity has been effective in supplying accurate information. This material lends itself to further practice activities, such as students testing each other, a discussion on the relative usefulness of the gadgets, personalisation, etc. Students can also make use of the 'enabling language' (i.e. 'What's the thing you use for ...?') to ask about other items which they do not know in English and which they would like to know.

5.2.2 USING A DICTIONARY

If the student has no teacher or peer to ask, he can still solve a number of problems by using a dictionary. This could be a dictionary specially written for foreign students (recommended dictionaries are on page 101) or a bilingual dictionary. Historically, dictionaries have had a rather varied press according to the current thought on methodology. Bilingual dictionaries were frowned upon, particularly in the 1960s and early 1970s, when methodology swung away from translation as an approach to language learning. It must also be said that many bilingual dictionaries (and to some extent, EFL dictionaries) tended to be unreliable and at times inaccurate; these criticisms can still be levelled at some of them. Further, in the late 1970s, many teachers were suspicious of the use of dictionaries, feeling that this was synonymous with laziness on the part of the student who was unwilling to use his own resources and guess the meaning for himself.

The criticisms above all have some validity, but it is important at the same time to consider certain advantages in the use of dictionaries. A learner who makes good use of a dictionary will be able to continue learning outside the classroom, and this will give him considerable autonomy about the decisions he makes about his own learning. In the very early stages of learning, even an inadequate bilingual dictionary in a foreign country is better than nothing at all; it can provide important support and be a quick way of finding information.

Another way in which the dictionary is a valuable support is as a backup to contextual guesswork. It is not uncommon for an item in a particular context to appear ambiguous, and in such cases, the

<u>*EFL DICTIONARIES*</u> – *Some useful features to highlight for students*

Pronunciation

Teach students to recognise *phonemic script* and illustrate *stress marking* in the dictionary to enable them to become self-sufficient in finding out how to pronounce items. This can be done gradually. The dictionary will also give guidance on stress on two-word compounds and idioms and the pronunciation of derivatives and inflections.

Grammar

It may be necessary to point out to the students the abbreviations used for the following parts of speech.
Verb patterns: whether verbs are transitive or intransitive, followed by infinitive or gerund, 'that' clause, preposition, etc.
Irregularity: plurality of nouns, comparative/superlative of adjectives, past tense and past participle of verbs.
Separability of phrasal verbs.
Countability of nouns.

Writing

Spelling: plurality of nouns, doubling of consonants on verbs and adjectives, US versus GB spelling.
Word division.
The *OALDCE* has an appendix on punctuation.

Meaning

Definitions are generally listed in order of frequency (but proceed with caution).
The items are contextualised to illustrate usage.
Guidance is given on style (e.g. pejorative, slang) and register (e.g. chemical, engineering).
Meaning of idioms, multi-word verbs and proverbs is given.
The illustrations in the dictionaries are sometimes quite useful in the classroom, though they are often idiosyncratic and specialist material.

Recommended dictionaries are on page 101.
Use Your Dictionary (Underhill, 1980), is an extremely useful and well-organised book designed to train learners to use dictionaries effectively.

dictionary is an important resource to clarify the uncertainty. Consider the following example:

He went to a school where the policy was to allow students to make their own decisions about whether or not to attend lessons. They were actively encouraged to consider this carefully. In his particular case, he *loafed* for three years before he made up his mind to go to the car maintenance class.

In the example, 'loafed' might mean 'to do nothing' or perhaps 'to consider' if looked at from the learner's point of view. The dictionary would allow him to solve the ambiguity. There are of course occasions when contextual guesswork is impossible, and a dictionary may be the only study aid available.

It is also worth pointing out two further considerations which are characteristic of many teaching and learning situations. A lot of students (whether prompted to do so by their teachers or not) are likely to have recourse to dictionaries, and in many cases these are tiny bilingual dictionaries which do little more than give one word equivalents and are often very inaccurate. It seems worth tapping this innate desire for a reference work by showing students how, in effect, a well-designed dictionary can be of greater benefit to them. Secondly, while no one would claim that EFL dictionaries are perfect, (see ch. 1, activity 3) a student is just as likely to find an appropriate answer or confirmation of his guesses in a dictionary as elsewhere; in other words, dictionaries seem to be as accurate as peer learners or even teachers, and in many cases, more so.

In a learning situation, therefore, dictionary training should be an integral part of any syllabus and we include here a list of the particular features of a foreign learner's dictionary which make it such a useful aid.

One specific feature of the dictionary which provides a valuable learning tool is the use of phonemic transcription and stress marking, and students who become proficient at recognising these will be even more self-sufficient. Below are two exercises which have two distinct teaching aims in each case. They both have a lexical aim (i.e. they outline an area of vocabulary to be learnt) and they also aim to develop an awareness in the learner of a particular aspect of vocabulary learning which a good dictionary will highlight.

STUDENT ACTIVITY

Multi-word verbs

With some multi-word verbs, the two parts of the verb can be separated, but with others they cannot.

Separable	*Inseparable*
e.g. I *turned on* the TV. √	e.g. I *looked after* | them.
I *turned* the TV *on*. √	| the children. √
I *turned* it *on*. √	I *looked* the children *after*. ✗
	I *looked* them *after*. ✗

This difference is indicated in the dictionary by the way the verb is entered:

e.g. to turn *sth*. on   e.g. to look after *sb*.

to turn *sth*. off   to get over *sb*./*sth*.

to try *sth*. on   to look into *sth*.

(sth. = something   sb. = somebody)

Read the following sentences and try to guess the meaning of the verbs. Write your answer next to the sentence.

1 It's a difficult exam but I think I'll *get through*.

2 This handwriting is so bad I can't *make out* what it says.

3 You should *look up* a word in the dictionary if you don't know the meaning.

4 You have to write something, so if you don't know the correct answer, you will have to *make up* something.

5 You'd better *note down* that final point or you might forget it.

6 I didn't really understand your lesson on the present perfect, so could we *go over* it again?

Now use your dictionary for two reasons:

a) to check the meaning and see if you were right. Remember, there may be more than one meaning, so look at all the definitions and then at the sentence again before you decide which definition is correct.

b) find out if the verbs are separable or inseparable. Make a note of them as we do at the top of the page (e.g. to turn *sth*. off).

© 1986 Cambridge University Press

STUDENT ACTIVITY

The following all have one phonemic sound in common. What is it? Write the words in phonemics and in normal English next to the picture (in each case the first *phonemic* symbol has been given to help you).

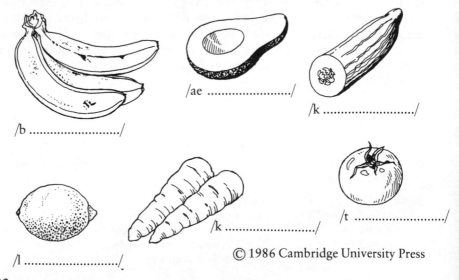

/ae ..../

/k ..../

/b ..../

/k ..../

/t ..../

/l ..../

© 1986 Cambridge University Press

5.2.3 CONTEXTUAL GUESSWORK

This involves making use of the context in which the word appears to derive an idea of its meaning, or in some cases to guess from the word itself. In the case of the latter, speakers of Romance languages and Germanic languages have an obvious advantage as so many words are almost identical, in form if not pronunciation, to words in their own language. There will be occasions when this similarity is very misleading, and in many cases the English meaning will only approximate to the word in the student's mother tongue. Nevertheless it is still a great advantage and one that should be exploited.

Speakers of European and non-European languages alike can also make use of their previous knowledge of English to guess the meaning of new words. Consider the new lexis encountered by an intermediate student in the following examples:

1 I *overslept* this morning.
2 My work *varies* from week to week.

In the first example the new word comprises parts that are already familiar and the student might also have met the same prefix in other words e.g. overtime. This knowledge should enable the student to work out the meaning. In the second example the student's knowledge of the more common noun 'variety' may be sufficient to deduce the meaning of 'varies' and understand the sentence.

Many teachers devise classroom activities to develop the ability to guess from context, one of the most common being the substitution of a nonsense word for a particular item in order to make the students focus on the context to decide exactly what is being substituted:

e.g. Can you turn the *zong* on, it's cold in here?

After the students have guessed that a 'zong' is some form of heater, the exercise could be extended to sensitise students to the importance of the grammar of the item and prefixes/suffixes as a clue to meaning:

e.g. This particular dish cannot be *rezonged*.

Following on from this type of exercise where the target word is clearly isolated, one can approach denser texts in which a wider context needs to be understood before the meaning of a single item surfaces:

e.g. The newspaper has suffered during the past year because advertising money has fallen by ten per cent. However, this fall has been *offset* by increasing the price of the paper from 20 pence to 22 pence.

'Offset' here means: (a) made worse, (b) made better, (c) balanced.

This example illustrates the importance of understanding discourse markers, in this case 'however', to deduce meaning. It should also be possible to guess the meaning even if we distract the students by surrounding the target item with more unknown vocabulary:

e.g. The newspaper has suffered a number of setbacks during the past year, the most important being the ten per cent fall in advertising revenue. However, the decline has been offset by the pricing policy which raised the profit margin for each newspaper sold.

The ability to guess from context is clearly a valuable skill and one that should play a part in textual exploitation in class. It should be remembered, though, that there are students for whom contextual guesswork is an obvious strategy and one that does not require a lot of time spent on it. Other students may have considerable difficulty with this type of task and would need to have the skill developed more gradually. This leaves the teacher with the problem once again of different skills and needs, and reinforces the need for student-centred activities allowing some flexibility in the nature of the task.

It is also important that contextual guesswork is not introduced into the lesson at a time when other skills are being developed. Classroom cassette recorders permit students to rewind and focus on a particular word or phrase, but this is not a facility that is available in real situations where time spent deciding the meaning of a single item probably results in the listener missing the next three sentences. In these situations attention to detail can reinforce certain students' obsession with understanding every word and have a detrimental effect on global understanding. The same is true of written texts. Lengthy deliberations on a single item will interfere with the development of the skill of 'gist' reading.

Finally it must be emphasised that students should not be asked to guess the meaning from context when the context is wholly inadequate to the task. With hindsight it is all too easy to see how the context illuminates the meaning of the target item; from a position of ignorance it is not always that simple. This is particularly true if the target item is surrounded by additional items which may be unknown or only partially known to the students.

The following activity begins with an exercise to test general understanding of the passage, and then requires the students to make use of the map and text to guide them towards an understanding of the target language. The consolidation exercises permit quite a lot of freedom, and certain steps can be omitted if the students are finding it easy.

STUDENT ACTIVITY

An accident

a) Read the article 'Smash girl in a tizzy', then look at the two maps at the bottom of the page and choose the map which corresponds to the article.

b) Now look at your map again and mark the following:
   a roundabout
   a pedestrian crossing
   a junction

Smash girl in a tizzy

MOTORIST Lesley Aston doesn't remember much about her trip home from work.

But villagers at Studley, Warwicks, will never forget it.

First, her Austin 1300 rammed the back of another car waiting at a junction.

She drove off without stopping, overtook cars waiting at a pedestrian crossing and swung into a roundabout on the wrong side.

Then 20-year-old Lesley crashed head-on into a second car, swerved into a third and careered into a brick wall before coming to rest on a garage forecourt.

She later told police that she had only vague memories of what had happened, magistrates were told yesterday at Alcester, Warwicks.

Lesley, of Hewell Road, Redditch, Worcs., was fined £150 for reckless driving and failing to stop after an accident or report it.

(from the *Daily Mirror*)

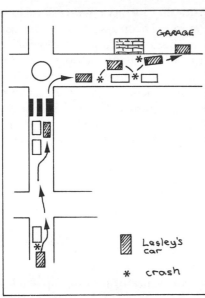
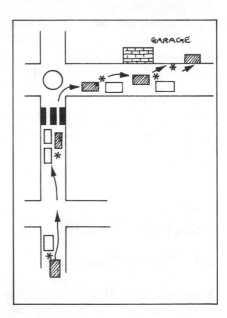

Lesley's car

* crash

c) Read the following account of an accident and draw what happened.

Car A tried to overtake car B approaching a road junction. Car C which was coming in the opposite direction swerved to avoid car A and crashed into a tree near the corner of the junction.

d) Read the article again and try to guess the meaning of the following:
rammed (para 3)
vague (para 6)
reckless (para 7)

Write an account of an accident yourself. Read it out to your partner while he or she draws it.

85

6 Memory and written storage

Understanding how we store information in the memory and why certain chunks of it seem to 'stick' while others slip away is obviously a matter of concern to anyone whose work involves helping others to learn. For language teachers this knowledge should help to establish classroom procedures that will promote more effective learning and retention of new language items.

These are the issues we will be considering in this chapter, but first a word about the organisation of the chapter. The first section is devoted to theoretical aspects of memory but is both brief and selective. We have tried to define and outline only those aspects of memory that are particularly relevant to the later discussion, and provide the necessary background to allow a more objective assessment of certain classroom activities. The sections on classroom suggestions and written storage take up the practical aspects more explicitly but also contain descriptions of scientific experiments that we have found interesting and relevant to classroom teaching.

THEORETICAL ASPECTS

6.1 Types of memory

Most readers will be familiar with the experience of looking up a telephone number and then repeating it to themselves for the time it takes to sit down and dial the number. As luck would have it, this is invariably the occasion for somebody to ask a distracting question with the result that the number is forgotten and has to be looked up all over again. Equally familiar and irritating is when you need the same number twenty-four hours later and find that you are quite unable to remember it.

These experiences reflect the widely recognised view among psychologists that with verbal learning the ability to hold information over brief periods (usually up to thirty seconds in duration) demands fairly constant repetition, and any distraction or interruption is likely to severely impede that ability. Moreover, it has been established that our capacity for short term retention is remarkably consistent, and that most people experience some breakdown in retention as soon as the number of items or chunks of information exceeds seven.

This type of memory, known as *short term memory*, is clearly different from *long term memory*, which is our capacity for recall of information minutes, weeks and years after the original input. Furthermore the difference is not simply one of duration. Unlike short term memory which is limited in capacity, long term memory is seemingly inexhaustible and can accommodate any amount of new information. Not surprisingly this additional information can only be stored at a price; it is generally acknowledged that we need to work much harder to commit information to long term memory, and the type of repetition we described as being essential to short term retention may not be adequate for long term retention.

Some readers may feel uneasy about this last comment, as it would seem to contradict an experience we have all shared, namely the ability to remember certain information either by means of repetition, or with no conscious attempt to learn it at all. This certainly does happen, and the distinction between short term retention and long term retention is not always clear-cut. Information entering short term memory may pass quite effortlessly into long term memory, and some learners may find repetition a very effective way of transferring information into long term memory. Later in the chapter we will take up the issue of repetition in more detail; at this stage we will simply acknowledge it has a role in long term learning but reiterate the importance of more thorough processing and systematic organisation as the basis for effective long term retention.

6.2 Organisation of the mental lexicon

In part A of this book, we looked at the relationships between lexical items and other linguistic considerations such as pronunciation, grammatical values, derivation, spelling, etc. All this information is stored in the brain, so we should now examine *how* this data is organised and stored.

Our 'mental lexicon' is highly organised and efficient. Were storage of information haphazard, we would be forced to scan in a random fashion to retrieve words; this simply is not feasible when one considers the speed at which we need to recognise and recall. Furthermore, it is extremely improbable that we organise words in the brain as a dictionary does. Imagine you were trying to recall the word 'nozzle', for instance. It is unlikely that you would retrieve the word 'noxious' (which appears next to 'nozzle' in the *LDCE*) in place of the target word.

Some very interesting experiments carried out by Brown and McNeil

(1966) exemplify this point forcefully and give us clues about lexical organisation. The experimenters gave testees definitions of low frequency vocabulary items and asked them to name the item. One definition was, 'A navigational instrument used in measuring angular distances, especially the altitude of the sun, moon and stars at sea'. Some testees were able to supply the correct answer (which was 'sextant'), but the researchers were more interested in the testees who had the answer 'on the tip of their tongues'. Some gave the answer 'compass', which seemed to indicate that they had accessed the right semantic field but found the wrong item. Others had a very clear idea of the 'shape' of the item, and were often able to say how many syllables it had, what the first letter was, etc. It seems, then, that these systems are interrelated; at a very basic level, there appears to be a phonological system, a system of meaning relations and a spelling system.

One way in which researchers investigate how the mental lexicon is organised is by comparing the speed at which people are able to recall items. It is generally accepted that if certain types of prompts can be answered more quickly than others, then this will reflect the lexical system. Freedman and Loftus (1971) asked testees to perform two different types of tasks:

e.g. 1 Name a fruit that begins with a p.
  2 Name a word beginning with p that is a fruit.

Testees were able to answer the first type of question more quickly than the second. This seems to indicate that 'fruits beginning with p' are categorised under the 'fruit' heading rather than under a 'words beginning with p' heading. Furthermore, experimenters discovered in subsequent tests that once testees had access to the 'fruit' category, they were able to find other fruits more quickly. This seems to provide further evidence that semantically related items are 'stored together'. Most researchers (albeit from varying viewpoints) appear to agree that items are arranged in a series of associative networks. Forster (1976, 1979) put forward the theory that all items are organised in one large 'master file', and that there are a variety of 'peripheral access files' which contain information about spelling, phonology, syntax and meaning. Entries in the master file are also held to be cross-referenced in terms of meaning relatedness.

We also have to consider other variables which affect storage. One important factor here is *word frequency*; items which occur most frequently are also easily recognised and retrieved. Imagine a pile of cards, each representing an item of vocabulary. In this system, the most frequently used items are 'at the top of the pile', and therefore easier to retrieve. *Recency of use* is another variable, and, to return to the analogy of the pile, one can imagine words more *recently* used being at the top. These variables are concerned with the use of items, but it is also important to consider when items were first *learnt*. Imagine a pile of words organised chronologically: the words learnt on the first day of a course would be at one extreme and those most recently learnt at the other.

Clearly, native speakers do not acquire all their vocabulary in lexical sets, but rather acquire items in a haphazard, chronological fashion, generally in a fairly predictable order of frequency. However, native speakers have many years in which to build up a comprehensive lexicon, whereas foreign learners are limited in this respect. Exploiting our present knowledge of storage systems to the full should allow us to attempt to speed up the learning process and facilitate storage. This will be true whether we are trying to clarify associative networks, classify by categories or organise the vocabulary syllabus in a way which will assist the contribution of frequency and recency of use and other variables. We will discuss the practical implications of this in the second part of this chapter.

6.3   Why do we forget?

In spite of the efficiency of these various organisational networks in the memory, we still suffer lapses when we are unable to remember something that we thought was well established in our long term memory. Why does this happen?

One theory of forgetting suggests that information stored in the memory falls into disuse unless it is activated fairly regularly. In other words, we need to practise and revise what we learn otherwise the new input will gradually fade in the memory and ultimately disappear. This is called the *decay theory*.

In opposition to this theory is the notion of *cue-dependent forgetting*, which asserts that information does in fact persist in the memory but we may be unable to recall it. In other words, the failure is one of retrieval rather than storage. Evidence for this theory resides in a number of experiments. In one of these, subjects were given lists of words to learn and then tested on their powers of recall. Later they were tested again, only this time they were given relevant information to facilitate recall. For example, if a list contained the words 'sofa', 'armchair' and 'wardrobe', the subjects would be given the superordinate 'furniture' as a cue to help them. These experiments showed that recall was considerably strengthened by appropriate retrieval cues, thus suggesting that the information was not permanently lost but only 'mislaid'.

In addition to the theories of decay and cue-dependent forgetting there is further evidence that any significant mental activity undertaken before or after periods of learning can also account for poor learning and retention. The activities undertaken prior to learning may have a detrimental effect on our ability to absorb new input, while activities undertaken after periods of learning can interfere with the effective consolidation and retention of new input. How long this interference persists is difficult to determine but the effects are likely to be most acute in the hours immediately preceding or following periods of learning. This contrasts with 'decay' which is obviously more significant in accounting for memory failure over a long period of time.

One final point about forgetting is the rate at which we forget. It is generally believed that of the information we forget, eighty per cent is lost within twenty-four hours of initial learning. This may help to explain why testing activities carried out the day after input may yield rather distressing results, while further testing activities carried out a week later appear quite satisfactory. This rate of forgetting clearly has implications for revision and recycling which will be discussed later.

As language teachers, our main concern is to ensure that what is taught will be permanently retained in long term memory, so it is clearly a matter of some importance that classroom activities take account of these various theories, and strive to combat decay and interference while developing and facilitating efficient retrieval systems.

PRACTICAL IMPLICATIONS

6.4 Meaningful tasks

Recent trends in methodology have stressed the need for meaningful activities in the classroom. There are a variety of reasons for this, among them the swing towards realism and authenticity and the need to engage learners in activities which will enable them to be more self-reliant. Equally important here is the fact that more meaningful tasks require learners to analyse and process language more deeply, which helps them to commit information to long term memory. The theory that a student's 'personal investment' has a very positive effect on memorisation is one that many teachers and learners will intuitively agree with.

An experiment by Wilson and Bransford provides an interesting insight here. In this experiment, three different groups of subjects were used. The first group were given a list of thirty words and told that they would be tested on their ability to recall the words. The second group were given the same list of words and told to rate each word according to its pleasantness or unpleasantness; they were *not* told that they would be tested on their ability to recall the words. The third group were given the list and asked to decide whether the items on the list would be important or unimportant if they were stranded on a desert island. They too were *not* told that they would be tested on these items. The results of the tests showed a similar degree of recall between groups one and two, while group three recorded the highest degree of recall. This experiment illustrates several important points:

1 That the intention to learn, however laudable, does not in itself ensure that effective learning will take place.
2 That subjects are more likely to retain verbal input (i.e. commit new items to long term memory) if they are actively engaged in a meaningful task that involves some kind of semantic processing, and provides a unifying theme to facilitate *organisation* in the memory.

To test some of these assertions, you could try the following experiment with your class. Divide the class in half and send one half out of the room. Tell the remainder that they must learn the following group of words:

aubergine (+ mother-tongue equivalent in all cases)
courgette   leek   cabbage
celery   swede   beetroot

(If any of these vegetables are not found in your country, you could change the item for another vegetable which will be familiar to your students although a new item for them in English.) Then instruct the second group that they must list the items in order of personal preference. At the end of the lesson, after an intervening activity, you could test both groups on their ability to recall the items.

Guided discovery is another way in which teachers can engage the students' interest and involve them in a level of semantic processing which should promote more effective learning and retention. An important qualifying statement here is that the students have the means to perform the learning task, otherwise they will become frustrated and lose motivation.

Consider the following methods of presenting the item 'to swerve'.

1 The teacher explains that 'swerve' is a verb and means to change direction suddenly. He exemplifies this on the board with the sentence 'the car swerved to avoid the child', and then conducts some drilling of the example sentence.
2 The teacher asks the question, 'Why would you swerve in a car?' The students are then supplied with dictionaries to look up the word 'swerve' and told to write their answer on a piece of paper.

The first presentation is probably quite adequate to convey the meaning of 'swerve', but the second approach may be more memorable for the learners. Not only does it involve an element of guided discovery, but it also engages the students in a degree of semantic analysis i.e. what causes somebody to swerve; this is not required of them in the first presentation.

6.5 Imagery

Teachers often make extensive use of visual images in the classroom for illustrating meaning. One further advantage of this is that our memory for visual images is extremely reliable and there is little doubt that objects and pictures can facilitate memory. Equally obvious is that it is easier to conjure up a mental image of a concrete item than an abstract one; try, for instance, to 'image' the following: 'bottle', 'dog', 'truth', 'life'. You will probably have had no difficulty with the first two, but it is extremely difficult to supply a visual image for 'truth' and 'life'.

Our ability to produce mental images has led to a memory technique known as the *key word technique*. It consists of associating the target word with a word which is pronounced or spelt similarly in the mother tongue, but is not necessarily related in terms of meaning.

e.g. *Rathaus* (German, meaning 'town hall') sounds like 'rat house' in English.

The learner then conjures up a visual image of a lot of rats coming out of his local town hall, for instance. It appears to aid memory if the meaning and the key word are made to interact, as in the case above.

Some claims are also made that the more bizarre the image, the easier it will be to recall, but the evidence for this is unconvincing. We feel that this type of 'mnemonic' or memory aid has a very limited application. It may be particularly useful for certain types of learners (who may use it without prompting in any case) and we suspect that many learners make use of this in the very early stages of learning a language for a handful of items. The results of classroom trials (Fuentes, 1976) seemed to indicate that the use of key words did not produce higher recall than any other type of memory technique, including rote learning. We also feel that, if used exclusively, it approaches vocabulary learning in a very one-dimensional way and in effect fails to take into account most of the linguistic problems discussed in chapters 2 and 3, much in the same way as a traditional translation equivalent vocabulary list.

6.6 Rote learning

Another memorisation technique which has a long history in language learning is rote learning. This involves repetition of target language items either silently or aloud and may involve writing down the items (perhaps more than once). These items commonly appear in list form; typical examples being items and their translation equivalent (e.g. door = *die Tür*), items and their definitions (e.g. nap = short sleep), paired items (e.g. hot–cold, tall–short), and irregular verbs. A common practice is for the learner to use one side of the list as prompts and cover the other side in order to test himself.

In the early stages of language learning, repetition gives the students the opportunity to manipulate the oral and written forms of language items, and many learners derive a strong sense of progress and achievement from this type of activity. For this reason it can be very valuable. It may also be a very legitimate means of transferring items into long term memory where there is a direct mother-tongue equivalent and very little semantic coding is involved in the learning process. For universal paradigms such as days of the week, or for irregular verbs (as long as the meaning of the verb is known), a mechanical learning activity of this type may be quite useful.

However, earlier in this chapter we indicated that a far deeper level of processing is required to commit items to long term memory and we illustrated the type of processing that will be involved. In addition, lists of translation equivalents may be counter-productive for learners, as memorisation of this type may delay the process of establishing new semantic networks in a foreign language.

6.7 Recycling

The importance of recycling previously presented lexis is a direct consequence of the theories of forgetting, discussed in an earlier section. If memory traces do gradually fade in the memory without regular practice then it is clearly necessary that we create opportunities in the classroom for students to practise what they have learnt. And given that other learning activities will interfere with effective retention of new lexis, we should try to ensure that practice is carefully spaced and that students are not being overloaded with too much new lexis at any one time. This will be a function of the course designer as much as the teacher, but only the teacher can accurately measure the extent of recycling or the pacing of new input that will be appropriate for their students on a daily or weekly basis. With regard to the theory of cue-dependent forgetting, it will also be a function of recycling that students are being asked to locate items in their long term memory. Developing effective retrieval systems may not require lengthy practice and can easily be incorporated into the lesson by way of 'warmer' activities at the beginning. The teacher could, for example, give the students an appropriate retrieval cue for vocabulary presented in the previous lesson and see how many items the students can recall. Alternatively he could present the students with disparate items presented over several lessons and ask the students to organise them into different categories. Both activities are helping to assist the process of subjective organisation so essential to effective retention and recall.

As mentioned earlier the rate of forgetting also has implications for the recycling of lexical input. If eighty per cent of what we forget is lost within twenty-four hours, there is a strong argument for revising new language items one day after initial input. In *The Brain Book* (1979), Peter Russell actually sets out a revision schedule to ensure that new material is permanently recorded. His timetable is as follows:

1 A five-minute review five to ten minutes after the end of a study period.
2 A quick review twenty-four hours later.
3 A further review one week later.
4 Final reviews one month later and then six months later.

Such a detailed plan of campaign is unrealistic for most lexical items, unless teachers are fortunate enough in having course designers who have integrated systematic lexical recycling into the prescribed syllabus. However, it should still be possible for teachers to incorporate some of this organised recycling into their lessons. We have already advocated the regular use of warmer activities at the beginning of a lesson to aid recall and develop retrieval systems; in addition we would recommend that teachers try to include a quick review of important lexis one to two days after initial input. This should help to compensate for any decline in the memory trace, and combat the effects of interference which crowd the memory with new information, making it difficult to locate previously learned lexis. With regard to further recycling, weekly or monthly progress tests (the choice depending on course duration and intensiveness) are probably the easiest and most practical way of ensuring some check on previously learned lexis.

One final point about recycling is that it is not just a matter of quantity but also of quality. Although teachers provide example sentences for new lexical items they are not in the habit of illustrating the item with three or four different examples. They might argue that it would be too time-consuming to present so many examples, and in any case why give four examples when one will do? The problem of time is inescapable and there is a danger that varied examples can be overwhelming for the students and lead to more confusion than understanding. In the long term, though, students will find it easier to retain and retrieve an item from long term memory if they have been exposed to it through a number of different contexts. And this will be just as true for your own understanding of vocabulary teaching. Imagine reading this book four times. You may learn something on the second reading that you missed on the first, but you are unlikely to gain very much on the third or fourth readings. Compare that with reading four different books on the same subject where you have the opportunity to meet similar subject matter but each time seen from a slightly different point of view. Initially this may be confusing but eventually you will gain far more insight and depth of understanding, and this in turn will fix the ideas more permanently in your long term memory. Following the restricted contextualisation of new lexis for initial teaching purposes, it will therefore become a function of recycling to expand the context range of an item and so facilitate retention and recall.

6.8   Written storage systems for learners

Traditionally, most learners were encouraged to list vocabulary items as they were learnt in a chronological order. The most common way of indicating meaning was to assign a mother-tongue equivalent to each item – our French vocabulary notebooks looked something like this:

> L'arbre (m) = the tree
> léger (adj) = light
> écouter (v) = to listen
> etc.

Although this system gives us a very basic form of information about the most common meaning of an item as well as its part of speech and gender, the organisation represents a very one-dimensional view of language. It does not reflect the types of associations we have just discussed, and an arrangement like this is likely to present hurdles to the learner rather than facilitating the learning process. Lack of contextualisation will encourage the learner to assume that *léger* could be used in the context of 'a light room' (i.e. the opposite of dark) and this would be quite wrong. Moreover, this system of storage is not flexible; it does not allow for later additions or refinements as one's knowledge of the uses and derivatives of an item increases, and gives us no indication here of the pronunciation of the items. A more comprehensive framework is given below and it is important to encourage students to store items with the relevant information. They should also leave space so that they can add to the entry where need be:

murder (n) + (v) /ˈmɜ:də/ = to kill somebody by plan or intention against the law *

e.g. Jack the Ripper murdered lots of women.

*or a translation

PERSONAL CATEGORY SHEETS

Learners can store new vocabulary as it arises on appropriate category sheets which they can keep in a ring binder or on separate pages of a notebook. The sheets could have headings such as topic areas or situations, these headings being selected by the student himself. As he acquires new vocabulary, he can add to the sheets and cross-reference them where necessary. He will have to decide where to categorise and when to open a new category sheet. The information given on these sheets (i.e. meaning, perhaps translation, part of speech and an example) should be comprehensive as suggested above.

It is also possible for learners to use index cards; each card would contain information about lexical items and their derivatives, and the cards could be filed thematically. This is perhaps a rather cumbersome practice in the classroom, but may well suit individual learners for home use.

USING VISUALS

We mentioned the uses of diagrams and word trees in chapter 2 when discussing the teaching implications of sense relations. Visuals are an extremely useful framework for storage of lexis, and they can be used to highlight the relationships between items. Word field diagrams are of interest here and the example below (from *Use Your Dictionary*, Underhill, 1980) could be used as a testing activity by omitting some of the items. Learners could also be asked to organise their own diagrams of this type.

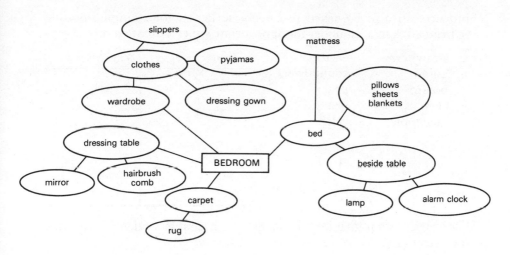

Trees can be used too:

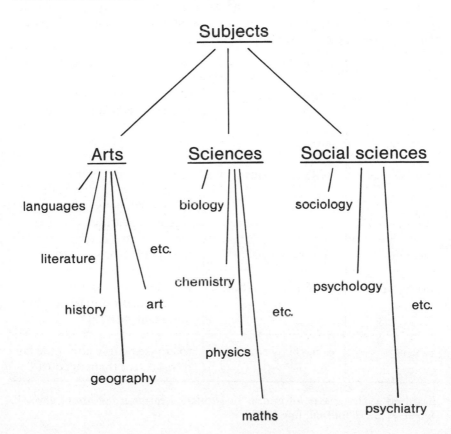

Students can also be asked to categorise items; for example, putting the hyponyms in a list under the appropriate superordinate term:

e.g. strawberry   carrot

		Fruit	*Vegetables*

onion   cauliflower
potato   peach
cherry   pea
pineapple   celery
pear

Dictionaries often give useful visuals which enable students to do this type of exercise.

The grid which follows could be done on the blackboard by the students themselves, after which they can copy down their own personal record of it. Alternatively, it can be done as a group or homework activity by giving the students only one column of information (perhaps the first) and asking them to supply the rest.

Profession	*Place of work*	*Duties*
surgeon	hospital/clinic	to operate on people to treat medical problems
mechanic	garage	to repair cars, lorries, etc.
plumber	buildings/houses	to put in and repair: – water pipes e.g. in bathrooms, kitchens, – central heating
foreman	factory/worksite	to supervise other workers
photographer	studio or anywhere	to take photos, commercially or artistically and to develop and print them
lawyer	office/law courts	to advise people about the law to represent them in court

(Based on a similar type of grid in *Vocabulary Learning: the use of grids*, P. D. Harvey, *ELT Journal*, July 1983.)

Giving students pictures with objects to label is clearly an effective form of storage; most course books contain useful visuals of this type and labelling can be a class or homework activity. Many students (not only children) enjoy drawing and it is worth exploiting this where possible as a storage device. It has the advantage both of the 'personal investment' of having drawn and labelled an item as well as being a simple and effective indication of meaning. (Whether the drawings are good or not is irrelevant; what matters is that they should be recognisable to the learner.)

ALPHABETICAL INDEX

Another way in which a learner may wish to organise items is alphabetically; the advantage of this is that it constitutes a 'personal dictionary' or record of items learnt up to that moment. This can be helpful for situations in which a learner *recognises* an item he has met before and entered in his storage system, but perhaps cannot remember its meaning or how it is used. However, if he has the *meaning* in his head but cannot remember how to express it, this system will not be at all helpful. An alphabetical card index could be compiled as a group effort by the class and teacher, and the index box kept in the classroom for the students to refer to when necessary. This could then provide useful backup for the personal category sheets (see above). Having a joint class index file will enable both teacher and learners to keep track on lexical items covered and provide simple materials for quick revision activities.

LABELLING

An amusing form of written storage which will also provide a great deal of inbuilt revision is labelling objects. Encourage your students to invest in a large packet of small adhesive labels, and as they learn new items of vocabulary, they can write them in phonemic script and roman script on to labels which they then stick to the appropriate objects in their homes. Every time a student opens his wardrobe door, for instance, he will see a label giving him the English version. Clearly, objects in the classroom can be labelled in the same way.

RANDOM ITEMS

A useful vocabulary revision activity is to write on the blackboard a number of vocabulary items which your students have learnt during the last few lessons. Jumble the words so that they do not appear on the blackboard in listed categories. Ask students to work alone to categorise the items into three or four groups. It is best if this type of organisation is subjective at least in the initial stages; it is important to allow the learners to make their own decisions about how they wish to arrange the items. Their groupings may be grammatical or semantic; they may wish to group items by colour, shape, function, pleasantness or unpleasantness, activity, etc. Once the students have organised the vocabulary in their own way, ask them to explain their grouping to the class or to discuss this in small groups. This can be a useful way of checking that the students have understood the items as well as providing an opportunity for them to store and organise subjectively.

SUMMARY

One aspect of storage which we have not mentioned so far is the way in which most learners note down lexical items as they occur i.e. chronologically. We are all familiar with the situation where a learner is trying to recall a lexical item and can probably remember approximately where on the page he wrote it, who his teacher was (if he has more than one) and, if a recently taught item, which day he first focussed consciously on it. In fact, we have almost certainly all experienced this first-hand. This reflects one aspect of memory which we should not neglect; our ability to recall items is often sparked off by trying to cast our minds back and visualise the time and place where we learnt something.

This chronological organisation is not incompatible with other forms of storage, such as categorical organisation, so we are not suggesting that this should be discouraged. The more systems a learner makes use of and the greater the exposure to target items, the easier it will be to retrieve from a variety of sources. Noting items chronologically in lessons and transferring this information to category sheets or card indexes at home seems a very worthwhile activity, and may suit certain types of learners. However, to be realistic, some learners may not be prepared to organise items in different ways, so the most helpful guidance teachers can give here, is to show learners how to be systematic whatever system they adopt. Being thorough about the information they record (as suggested at the beginning of this section) is one way. In addition, learners who wish to record items chronologically should be encouraged to keep one section of their notebook or file for vocabulary; to begin a new page for each separate lesson, to date each page and where possible to give it a heading. As organisation is the key to memory, this is an important part of teaching your students how to be efficient learners.

PART C CLASSROOM ACTIVITIES

The activities in this part of the book cover a wide range of ideas for presentation, testing, practice and revision but the central aim throughout remains the same: to find stimulating and generative activities in which the students will be using the target vocabulary. In addition, we have tried to ensure that most of the activities can be exploited at a wide range of levels so that you will be able to incorporate the ideas, if not the actual examples we provide, into your own teaching situation. But most important of all, we hope the material may act as a catalyst to trigger off further ideas of your own, thus making classroom vocabulary teaching a more enjoyable and satisfying experience for teacher and student alike.

Each activity in chapters 7–11 is described as follows: an indication of the appropriate level for the example given, instructions for classroom procedure (presentation and practice), and concluding comments which may offer a rationale for the activity and/or suggest ways of modifying the activity to suit different teaching environments. Material and instructions designed specifically for the students are clearly indicated and in most cases they precede the teacher's instructions for the activity. Unless otherwise stated, the activities can all be exploited at different levels simply by changing the target lexis.

In chapter 9 you will notice we have indicated a specific dictionary for most activities. For those readers not familiar with the abbreviated forms, the dictionaries are: *The Longman Active Study Dictionary of English (LASDE), The Longman Dictionary of Contemporary English (LDCE), The Longman Lexicon of Contemporary English (LLCE), The Oxford Advanced Learner's Dictionary of Current English (OALDCE).* These are certainly some of the most reliable dictionaries for foreign learners of English, and for any students pre-Cambridge First Certificate level we would particularly recommend the *Longman Active Study Dictionary.* Of course, these are not the only dictionaries that can be used, but it is essential when giving students a dictionary activity that the dictionary in question is adequate to the task. Our reference indicates one such dictionary but there may well be others, among them, of course, reputable bilingual dictionaries.

For many of the activities included here, you will need to make photocopies of the worksheets for your students. Note that some of the worksheets contain material that is not the copyright of the publisher of this book; it is therefore not possible to give permission to copy such worksheets. Those sheets that can legally be copied carry the wording '© 1986 Cambridge University Press'.

7 Using visual aids

Many teachers during their years of teaching build up a library of pictures; these may include wallcharts, commercially-produced flashcards, home-made magazine picture flashcards, hand-drawn pictures, and of course illustrations from course books and supplementary books. These aids can be used for presentation, practice, revision and testing. In this chapter, we intend to explore a variety of these aids which can be used to group items into coherent vocabulary lessons. We also hope to show how visual materials can be designed and exploited to illustrate the boundaries between words. Some of the exercises in this section aim to represent different types of sense relations diagrammatically; the word field diagram on hair and the cline on page 108 are two examples of this. Visual aids are also a very useful basis for language practice and we have tried to show how communicative practice can be achieved from clines, diagrams and grids as well as pictures.

7.1 Using pictures as a guide to meaning

i) WORD FIELD DIAGRAMS (see also p. 97)

Level: Upper-intermediate, advanced, though in principle this type of activity will suit any level above elementary.

Suggested procedure: Provide students with dictionaries and ask them to work in pairs or small groups. Either give them a copy of the diagram or ask them to copy it from the blackboard. Point out the progressions to them (i.e. hair being longer, shorter, etc.). Ask them to fill in the vocabulary items at the top of the page in the appropriate places on the diagram. When the students have completed this task, ask them to fill out their answers on the blackboard diagram. Discuss differences of opinion and standardise a correct diagram. Highlight any difficulties of pronunciation e.g. auburn. Point out that the layout is designed to highlight the most common order of adjectives before a noun.

Practice: Students take turns to describe a member of the group's hair without naming them or indicating their sex (e.g. 'This person has long, dark, wavy hair.'). The group then guesses which person is being described. If your group has little variation in hair colour or style,

The following adjectives can all describe hair. Fill in the circles and box and notice the progressions (e.g. longer–shorter).

frizzy   black   auburn   dark brown   long   blond   shoulder-length   curly
mousy   red   light brown   wavy   cropped   ginger   jet-black   mid-brown

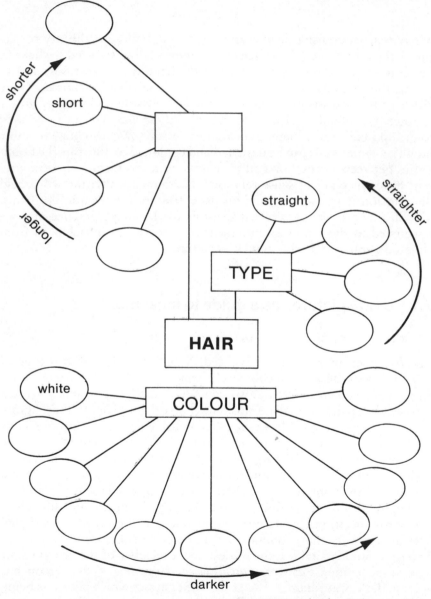

display a set of about twelve flashcards of famous people and ask students to describe one as above.

Comment: Students are asked here to use their shared knowledge of the language items, their dictionary skills and their knowledge of sense relations. It is a deceptively simple exercise.

ii)   VISUAL + TEXT

Level: Elementary.

Suggested procedure: Before using this material, you should revise 'colours' and pre-teach the items 'to match' and 'to go (well) with ...' (e.g. 'brown shoes go well with a beige suit').

   Give students a copy of the text and picture and explain that they should compare the text and the picture to deduce the meanings of the items 1–9 which are italicised in the text. They should write the numbers next to the respective items in the picture. Do the first example together, showing them the contextual clues which enable them to guess. Ask them to continue the activity in pairs or small groups. When they have finished, conduct a feedback session to clarify any problems, and highlight pronunciation difficulties at this stage.

Practice: The practice activities suggested underneath the text could be done in pairs or groups. Students could write a description of their own bedroom for homework.

Comment: This activity aims to show learners how to make use of contextual clues and to give them confidence to deduce meaning. Teachers could easily devise a written task of this type to accompany a wallchart.

This, as you can see, is my bedroom. It's full of modern furniture. I've got a single bed and I don't sleep very well on it because the *mattress* (1) is so hard and uncomfortable and it makes a noise. The *bedspread* (2) is covered with flowers and it's quite pretty, I suppose, but it doesn't look very nice with the two *rugs* (3) on the floor near the bed. I'd like to get one with the same design as the rugs. My landlady has given me an *alarm clock* (4) which I have next to the bed so that I wake up on time. I've got a *wardrobe* (5) in the corner and my landlady gets angry if I don't put my clothes in it. I put the smaller things like shirts and socks in the *chest of drawers* (6) (well, some-times I leave them on top of it). But it's a nice house, and my landlady changes the *sheets* (7) on the bed every week. Last week it was a lot colder so I asked her to give me an extra *blanket* (8). Oh, and one more thing about the bed: *pillows* (9) in England are very soft, so I need two for my head!

Practice: a) Look at the picture and decide on a colour scheme for the room.
b) Talk about your own bedroom at home.

iii) PICTURE CARDS

Level: Any level, provided learners know phonemic script.
Suggested procedure: Devise a series of cards as follows:

On one side of the card, show an illustration of the target item.
e.g.

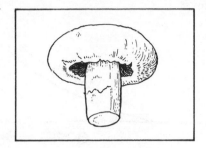 

On the other side, write the name of the item and transcribe into phonemic script:
e.g.

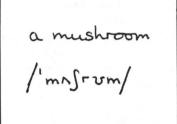 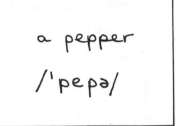

Give a card to each student. (If you want to teach seven to eight items, divide your class into the appropriate number of groups and duplicate the cards.) Check quickly that each individual student is able to pronounce the item with reasonable accuracy from the transcription.

Pre-teach: 'What's this called in English?'

Ask each student to hold his card so that only he can see the written words, while the others in the group can see the picture. Students then mingle and either have to identify the item if they know it, or ask the 'knower' what it is in English. The knower can then teach him the item. Impress on the students that they cannot sit down again until they can recall all the items in the group.

Comment: This activity allows the students the opportunity to pay greater attention to the items they find most difficult.

iv) SCALES AND CLINES

Level: From intermediate upwards, depending on the items the teacher chooses from those in the box. The set below would be suitable with advanced students.

Suggested procedure: Draw a line across the width of the blackboard and add the three items as follows:

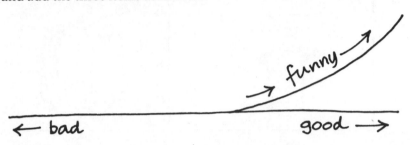

Make flashcards for each of the items you wish to select from the lists below, and give them to the students (perhaps one each, or one between two, etc., depending on the size of the class).

awful	hysterically funny	quite good
dreadful	mildly amusing	pretty good
not particularly good	a bit boring	superb
so-so	dire	fabulous
brilliant	quite funny	great
hilarious		

Ask students to stick their item (using Blutak if available) in the appropriate place on the line, having first consulted their dictionaries to check meaning if necessary. Ask the class to look at their final version together, discuss differences of opinion and then standardise a 'correct' version. Highlight any particular problems, such as pronunciation, (awful, dire), or the style of certain items (e.g. 'great' is fairly colloquial). Students should note down a copy of this line as a useful record of meaning.

Practice: Ask students to write the name of a book or play, spectacle and TV programme they are familiar with:

e.g. Book: *Papillon*
Film: *E.T.*
Spectacle: 'the football match between France and Italy on TV last night'
TV Programme: *Dallas*

Put them in pairs and ask them to tell their partner about these and their reactions to them. They should try to use the vocabulary from the lesson, but they will inevitably draw on other items from their productive vocabulary within this area.

Comment: This exercise exploits the students' knowledge of sense relations – in this case, gradable antonyms.

v) GRAPH

Level: For students of business or commercial English, intermediate; for general students if interested, advanced.

Suggested procedure: Pre-teach the lexical items contained in the two sets of information:

to stand at (a figure), to level off, to fall / rise by X%, to reach a peak, to fall sharply, to double.

The simplest way to teach these is to draw a graph on the blackboard to illustrate the meaning. Check that students know the past tense forms of the verbs 'to fall' and 'to rise', and highlight the preposition 'by' e.g. to fall *by* X%.

Practice: Ask the students to form pairs and to sit facing each other. Give graph A to one student and graph B to the other, and ask them not to look at each other's papers. Tell them to exchange the information at the bottom of their sheets; gradually they will be able to plot the information onto the graph. (If the students are having particular difficulty with it, tell them that in January 1978, sales stood at £50,000.) At the end, students A and B can compare their graphs and one pair can draw their copy onto the blackboard in a final feedback. For further practice, students can draw their own sales graphs, dictate them to each other and then write a description of the sales curve for homework.

⋙→

Classroom activities

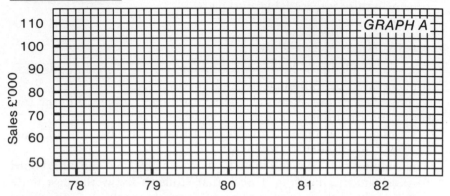

Information

1 In January 1980, sales were the same as January 1982.
2 In 1979, sales fell by almost 10,000.
3 In 1978, sales rose by 60%.
4 Sales doubled in the second half of 1980.
5 Sales reached a peak in June 1981 and then fell sharply for the rest of the year.

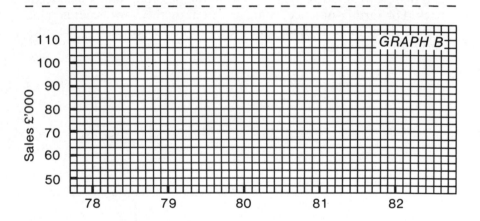

Information

1 In January 1982, sales stood at 70,000.
2 Sales levelled off in the first half of 1979.
3 In June 1980, sales were the same as in January 1978.
4 Sales rose by 50% between 1978 and the end of 1982.
5 Sales rose by 5% in the first half of 1981.

110

7.2   Using pictures for further practice

vi)   USING A WALLCHART

Level: Any.

Suggested procedure: 1 Choose a wallchart which your students have not seen before, containing vocabulary items you wish to revise with your class. Put the students in pairs and tell them the subject of the picture (e.g. a beach scene) but do not show it to them at this stage. Ask the students to predict which items of vocabulary they think are likely to arise. (In the case above, for instance, 'ice-cream', 'sand' and 'swimming costume' will probably be in the picture.) Conduct a feedback session during which you may wish to clarify any difficulties and correct errors of form and pronunciation.

2 Using the same pairs as before, ensure that one student in each pair is able to see the wallchart while the other student has his back to it, facing his partner. The students who cannot see the wallchart then ask whether their predictions were correct, while the other students confirm and add details:

e.g. Student B: Can you see any ice-creams? / Is anyone eating an ice-cream?

Student A: Yes, and there's a man selling ice-creams too.

This activity could be made into a competition in which students add up at the end the number of correct guesses.

vii)   PICTURE DICTATION

Level: Elementary upwards.

Suggested procedure: On the blackboard draw a large table with a dotted line down the middle. Thus:

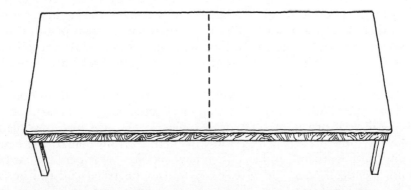

Ask the students to copy this drawing onto a sheet of paper. They will find it easier if they are equipped with pencils and rubbers.

Divide the class into two groups (A and B); give group A six items to draw on one side of their table, and give group B six different items to draw.

Make sure that each group can't see or hear what the other group has to draw.

Now ask the students in group A to find themselves a partner in group B and sit facing him.

Ask student B to fold over the half he drew on first so that student A cannot see it. Without showing his partner his own drawing, student A tells student B what to draw on his blank side of the table and where to draw it:

e.g. 'Draw a *tube of toothpaste* in the right hand corner ... no, that's too big – make it smaller ...', etc.

At the end, ask the pairs to compare their pictures.

Comment: Any concrete items can be used here, as long as they fit on a table. Apart from the vocabulary intended for revision, students will need to draw on other language e.g. comparatives. The same activity works well with landscapes, pictures of rooms, people, etc.

viii)   INFORMATION EXCHANGE VISUALS

Level: Elementary, but the type of activity is suitable for any level.

Suggested procedure: Find two pictures which are basically similar but have a certain number of differences between them. Pre-teach any items necessary (in this case, 'get in' versus 'get out', 'get on' versus 'get off', etc.). Put the students in pairs and ask them to sit facing each other. Show student A one picture and student B the other, and make it clear that they cannot look at their partner's picture. Tell them to describe to each other what is happening in their picture so that they can find the differences between the two pictures. It is useful to demonstrate to the class with one example first. At the end, conduct a feedback session where you can clarify problems, deal with errors, etc.

Comment: This activity is from *Play Games with English Book 1* (Granger, 1980) and *Book 2* contains exercises of a similar type, as does *Pair Work A & B* (Watcyn Jones, 1981). It is also possible to do the same activity with photos or pictures from magazines; many advertisements for products often have pictures which are similar but not identical. Many advertisements are symmetrical and can be cut down the middle to provide two similar pictures of cars, people, etc. We have found it extremely useful to build up a library of these paired pictures on a variety of topic areas.

Compare the pictures. Write what is different in picture B.

For example: In picture B . . .

The woman's opening her umbrella. It's raining.

(from *Play Games with English*)

ix) CUE CARDS

Level: Beginners upwards.

Suggested procedure: Find or make a set of pictures of items of everyday objects (e.g. newspaper, envelope, aspirin, toothbrush, stamps, apples, meat, bread). *Picture Cue Cards*, (J. K. Y. Kerr, 1979) are ideal for this type of activity, but you can of course use your own flashcards or realia.

Revise the vocabulary first and then, beginning with a picture which you show the class (e.g. aspirin), practise a short dialogue on the following lines:

A: Where are you going?
B: To the chemist's.
A: Why?
B: To get some aspirins.

Give each student a picture and ask the class to stand up and perform similar dialogues with each other. Tell them that once they have finished their conversation with a student, they should swap cards and find a new partner.

Comment: This is quite a standard and conventional exercise which provides valuable controlled practice; there are many useful and enjoyable activities of this type in the book which accompanies *Picture Cue Cards*. With this particular example, it is possible to revise two lexical areas at the same time: the objects and the shops.

Further reader activities

1 Design a word field diagram like the one on page 104 or the bedroom one on page 97 for one of the following:
height and bodyweight of a person
types of accommodation
contents of a living room
jumpers (colour, style, material)
2 Write a text to accompany any wallchart you use frequently, to encourage contextual guesswork on the lines of the exercise on page 105.
3 Design a scale or cline to illustrate one of the following: liking/disliking, big/small, adverbs of frequency.
4 Collect together a set of paired magazine pictures which have similarities and differences, and group them according to topic. Use them in the way suggested on page 112.

8 Using authentic reading texts

Written texts are often one of the major sources through which language learners meet new vocabulary, so it is only logical that they should be used extensively in classroom teaching. They have the great advantage of contextualising new language items for the learner, and an interesting text also serves to make that language more memorable.

Nevertheless texts are not always the ideal vehicle for vocabulary development in the classroom. One practical problem is length: interesting texts are often far too long for intensive study and can lead to considerable vocabulary overloading. The new lexis in a text will also be a very random selection, frequently defying any clear systematic organisation on the teacher's part, and containing many new items of marginal value to the students.

Perhaps the most barren feature of vocabulary exploitation in texts from published materials is the absence of exercises that activate useful lexis from the text. Questions testing receptive knowledge are common enough but productive practice activities even for useful high frequency items are rare. In our examples we have tried to include activities which will enable the teacher to integrate the new lexis with other skills work, and provide the students with productive language practice. The texts and accompanying tasks have also been chosen to illustrate and emphasise different types of exploitation, which include scanning, intensive study, prediction, contextual guesswork and word building.

i) FOCUSING ON KEY VOCABULARY IN A TEXT

Level: Intermediate.
Suggested procedure: Elicit from the students some of the things that can go wrong with holiday travel arrangements. Apart from generating interest for the text to follow, this will give you an idea of the vocabulary the students already know and an opportunity to introduce several new items they will meet in the text. The students then read the text and complete the true/false exercise individually or in pairs (with the help of a dictionary if necessary). Each question is designed to focus on particular target items, and those we have selected for attention are:

to go abroad	landing
to take off	damaged
to be delayed	ferry
to be held up	to cancel
to get off (a plane)	to go bust/bankrupt
to pick up (passengers)	to be off to ... (colloquial)

When you go through the answers you will need to clarify items that may have caused difficulty, and add further parts of speech to items encountered e.g. 'take-off' as a noun and verb. You should also check that your students know 'fly' (simple past and past participle), 'flight', 'suitcase', 'customs', 'fare', and 'booking'.

Practice: For further practice of these items see the role play on page 144.

<u>STUDENT ACTIVITY</u>

Read the following text and then answer the questions below.

LAURA'S HOODOO HOLS !

Mrs. LAURA LORD, Bacup, Lancs, writes:

I'VE been dogged by hoodoo holidays ever since I started going abroad twenty-three years ago. The first time I flew, the plane's radar failed, and we had to turn back and make an emergency landing.

When I was going to Tenerife, the plane was delayed two hours because punctures were found in the tyres.

Every year I buy a new case—not because I am extravagant but because, out of the millions of cases that go through customs, mine is the one that comes out damaged. In Holland, a coach party was held up for two hours because my case had been put on the wrong ferry.

In Bulgaria I had to buy a new case because mine was damaged beyond repair, but the zip broke and I ended up with a third case to bring my things home.

The year I went to Vancouver the tour company changed my booking seven times. I had wanted to fly from Manchester, but at the last minute the flight was changed to Gatwick.

After travelling all the

way down by train, we eventually took off—and landed in Manchester to pick up passengers!

When· I tried to claim back my rail fare to Gatwick I found the travel company had gone bust.

On top of all that, I suffer from acute angina and usually ask for low-level accommodation. But who always gets put on the top floor? Me!

This year I'm off to Yugoslavia—I think.

(from the *Daily Mirror*)

	True	False
1 Laura had her first holiday 23 years ago.		
2 The first time she flew there was an emergency; the plane's radar failed on the runway and the plane couldn't take off.		
3 When she went to Tenerife the plane took off two hours late.		
4 In Holland her coach party was delayed for two hours.		
5 In Holland she was delayed because her suitcase was put on the wrong boat.		
6 In Bulgaria she lost her suitcase.		
7 When she went to Vancouver her flight was cancelled.		
8 Her plane landed in Manchester so that passengers could get off.		
9 She couldn't get the money back for her train journey to Gatwick because the company had gone bankrupt.		
10 This year she is going to Yugoslavia.		

ii)   CONTEXTUAL GUESSWORK

Level: Lower-intermediate.

Suggested procedure: Follow the instructions on the student handout. This just leaves you with one important decision: when do you supply the missing words? You could write them on the blackboard (in no particular order) before you give the text to the students; this should enable the students to look up unknown items and complete the exercise successfully. With a monolingual group, though, it might be more interesting to see if the students can use the context to deduce the answer in their mother tongue, and then use a bilingual dictionary to find the English equivalent. If the results are unsatisfactory you will need to decide if the fault lies in the contextual guesswork or in the students' dictionaries.

Students can work on this activity individually or in pairs, and on completion you can conduct a group feedback in which you clarify any problems that might have arisen e.g. 'playing' would fit for number 8, but the instructions do state that each number represents a different

117

Read the texts below and see if you can supply the missing words. Altogether there are eight different items but some of them are repeated; each number represents a different item.

The show goes on

Diana Quick . . . delighted

....1.... Diana Quick accepted one of the biggest challenges in her career yesterday.

She took over the ...2... in Mindkill, the new £50,000 ...3... threatened by the sudden—and bitter—departure of Jill Bennett after a row over the script. The ...4... of ITV's Brideshead Revisited has only ten days to learn a 100-page ...5... that will put her on ...6... for all but three minutes of the 2½-hour ...3....

The play will open on August 7 at the Greenwich ...7...., London.

(from *The Standard*)

STAR: Noele

Brave Noele is back

....1.... Noele Gordon is back on ...6.... only nine months after beating cancer.

Noele—who played Meg Richardson in Crossroads for 18 years—is ...8.... a ...4.... role in the musical No No Nanette, which opens next week at Plymouth's ...7..... Royal.

The show lasts for more than two hours and Noele will be on ...6.... for much of the time, although she is still feeling the effects of her stomach cancer operation.

She said yesterday "My doctor has told me to go right ahead."

(from the *Daily Mirror*)

1	5 ....
2	6 ....
3	7 ....
4	8 ....

item. So, if the answer to number 3 is 'play', the answer to number 8 cannot be 'playing'. The answer in fact is 'rehearsing'.

Practice: Incorporating all of the items into a single activity is not easy, but the following ideas should enable you to concentrate on those that you consider to be most important for your particular group.

1 Put the students into groups and ask them to put the following information into the correct chronological order:

find a theatre
rehearse the play
find a director
select the actors/actresses for the minor parts
perform the play
find a play
actors/actresses learn their part
select (an) actor(s)/actress(es) for the star role(s)

2 Extend the lexical set by introducing some comparable cinema vocabulary e.g. to film, the set, on the screen; and then ask the students to compare making a film with performing a play. From an actor's point of view which do they think is easier, and which would they prefer to do? They should give reasons for their answers.

3 Compile a short quiz for your students based around a weekly magazine giving information about television programmes:

e.g. How many plays have been on television so far this week?
Who was the star of . . .?
Who played the lead in . . .?
How many actresses are there in . . .?

Students can answer the questions in groups, using their shared knowledge of the television programmes. Afterwards they can use the magazine to check their answers and find out the answers to any questions they didn't know. You can extend the activity further by getting the students to set their own questions.

Comment: Using two parallel texts gives students an opportunity to see the lexical items contextualised in a slightly different way; this enables them to test and consolidate their understanding of the target vocabulary.

iii) PREDICTING AND ACTIVATING VOCABULARY

Level: Intermediate.

Suggested procedure: Pre-teach 'fringe benefits' and then write the following fringe benefits on the blackboard. As you do so, you can ask members of the class to explain/guess what they are; you can explain any new items.

1 Staff canteen.

2 Cash incentives e.g. bonus payments, overtime opportunities.
3 Pension scheme.
4 Longer holidays.
5 Flexible working hours.

Practice: Put the students into small groups and ask them to decide on their order of priority for these benefits. When they have reached a consensus they can read the text and answer the questions.

Comment: Many course books use texts to present vocabulary but then fail to provide practice activities for the new vocabulary. This activity reverses the process. The teacher presents the new items and provides initial practice, the text is used for consolidation purposes and to provide a framework for further practice.

Holidays go to top of the perks list

by Sue Thomas

MORE CASH and the time to spend it are still more attractive to office workers than fancy fringe benefits like canteens, cheap loans, medical insurance and company social clubs, according to a report published today.

Longer holidays were top of the most wanted perk list when the Alfred Marks job agency questioned 1000 office staff on the subject.

Second in line were cash incentives and bonus payments, followed by flexible working hours.

Cash tomorrow gets very low priority, though. Pensions are almost bottom of the list of 13 common perks—regarded as less important than staff canteens and hairdressing allowances.

A wider survey of 382 companies employing 100,000 staff shows that many firms have lengthened holidays in the past few years, so that four weeks plus is now the norm. This compares with 17 days in 1975.

And more than half the firms questioned pay cash incentives or bonuses ranging from a few pounds up to nearly a third of annual salary.

Help with travel continues to increase, and nearly half the companies questioned give season ticket loans.

(from *The Standard*)

1 Is your order of priority for the five fringe benefits different from the text? If yes, what is the difference?
2 How many other fringe benefits does the text actually name? Underline them.
3 What do you think 'perks' are?
4 The text talks about thirteen fringe benefits. Not all of these are mentioned by name in the text. What do you think the missing fringe benefits might be?

iv) CONTEXTUAL GUESSWORK AND WORD BUILDING

Level: Upper-intermediate, particularly for students preparing for an examination in English.

Suggested procedure: To stimulate interest in the topic, begin by giving your students a very brief dictation (about three to four lines) to revise something you have done with them recently. Then ask them in groups to look at each other's papers and discuss the quality of the writing: whether it is tidy, easy to read, nice to look at, etc. They could also discuss the importance of handwriting as an introduction to the article. Before giving them the text, check that they know 'to pass/fail an exam' ('pass' is a false cognate in this context in several languages).

Give them the text and ask them to answer question 1. This is quite a complex text, so it is important to help them find the main point of it. The students can then complete sections 2 and 3 in pairs or groups, sharing their knowledge and using dictionaries. Teachers will probably wish to conduct a feedback session where they can discuss the answers and highlight difficulties of pronunciation or meaning and may also wish to deal more thoroughly with prefixation (especially 'il+' before adjectives beginning with 'l' and 'ir+' for adjectives beginning with 'r').

Practice: Ask students to discuss in groups the essay 'My cat'. They have been given a framework for discussion which uses the vocabulary taught in the lesson.

STUDENT ACTIVITY

EDUCATION

These extracts are from three identical essays. Why did two fail?

YOUR child could fail an examination solely because of his handwriting even when the examiners are not supposed to take it into account.

The illustration shows an extract from an essay written in three different styles of handwriting. Although the content was identical, the marks (given in percentages) were very different and made a difference between passing and failing. The only explanation is that, though none of the styles is illegible, the examiners found

⇶→

121

Sometimes it is possible. to tell a child who comes from a poor background even when the are wearing school uniform but it is not so	**STYLE ONE** **63–pass**
well. Sometimes it is possible to tell a child who comes from a poor background even when they are wearing school uniform but it	**STYLE TWO** **46–fail**
Sometimes it is possible to tell a child who comes from a poor background even when they are wearing school uniform but is is not	**STYLE THREE** **43.–fail**

style one neater and more attractive—and awarded extra marks.

The extracts come from an experiment carried out by Open University tutor Dennis Briggs, which is reported in the latest issue of Educational Review. Briggs took five different essays on the topic of school uniform, written by 16-year-old children in a recent English exam, and had each of them copied in five different handwriting styles.

There were now 25 different examples. These were handed out to 125 teachers, mostly English specialists working in secondary schools and, therefore, just the kind of people who would be marking exams at this level. Each teacher got five of the papers; none of them marked two examples of the same essay or of the same writing style.

Briggs then looked at the marks awarded by the teachers to each essay. As expected, some essays were consistently marked higher than others because of their content. But, just as often, essays identical in content were getting different marks.

In fact, there was almost as much variation between marks awarded to the same essays as between those awarded to different essays.

And the reason was the handwriting. All five essays got, on average, high enough marks for an O level pass when written in style one in our illustration. Yet four out of five failed when written in style two. One essay got on average, more than half as many more marks when style one rather than style three was used.

The implication is alarming: handwriting can make nearly as much difference as content to a child's marks.

The markers were not told to take handwriting into account. They were instructed to look at the quality of the ideas and the way they were expressed and at the choice of words. In the exam itself, children were told that "credit will be given for relevant ideas, use of appropriate language, careful spelling and punctuation." Again, there was no mention of handwriting.

" It looks very much," concludes Briggs, " that the 16-year-old who can present an essay one way will do better perhaps much better, than a friend who presents exactly the same literary standard but does not,·¹ or cannot, make it look so attractive."

Peter Wilby

(from *The Sunday Times*)

1 Look at the following paragraphs in the text and say which one most *clearly* explains the main idea of this article.
   a) Paragraph 3 ('The extracts come . . .')
   b) Paragraph 5 ('Briggs then looked . . .')
   c) Paragraph 8 ('The implication is . . .')
   d) Paragraph 10 ('It looks very much . . .')

2 Now find the words in the text for the following:
   From paragraph 2
   a) a piece of writing on a subject .*an essay*..........
   b) the ideas expressed in a piece of writing ....
   c) *now writt* is an example of bad ....
   d) impossible to read .... ⎤
   e) tidy .... ⎬ (adjectives)
   f) nice to look at .... ⎦

   From paragraph 9 ('The markers . . .')
   a) Hes going to fail isnt he This is a sentence with no ....
   b) He's failed agen hasen't he? This is a sentence with bad ....
   c) correct or acceptable in a given situation .... ⎤
   d) connected with the subject or topic .... ⎬ (adjectives)
   e) showing attention to detail .... ⎦

3 Look again at the adjectives above. In most cases, you can use a prefix or
   suffix to form the opposites. Study the list below.
   >   legible – *il*legible
   >   attractive – *un*attractive
   >   relevant – *ir*relevant
   > appropriate – *in*appropriate
   >   careful – care*less*
   >   neat – *un*tidy

   Now choose one of the words from the list above to fill the gaps.
   a) The presentation of his essay was rather .... so his teacher made
       him copy it out again.
   b) I couldn't read the letter because the handwriting was ....
   c) It is usually .... to call your boss 'darling'.
   d) He lost a lot of marks because the ideas he discussed weren't
       .... to the essay.
   e) There are too many .... spelling mistakes, I'm afraid.
   f) My handwriting used to be very untidy, but after reading this article, I'm going
       to try and make it ....

Practice: Look at the essay on the next page, written by an English child. In
   pairs, give marks out of ten for each of the following:
   out of ten for each of the following:
   Content: relevant Ideas?
   Choice of language: appropriate?
   Presentation: neat? attractive?
   Spelling: careful?
   Handwriting: attractive? legible?
   Punctuation: acceptable?

⫸→

Essay - My Cat

Cats are mysterius creatures they live in there own world and they are usually very independ ant. they like hunting buds and mice but they are also very fond of siting and sleepping in the sunshine a cat spends a lot of time just staring into space and proberbaly thinking about what its going to eat next

i wouldnt mind being a cat really becos nobody can tell you what to do.

© 1986 Cambridge University Press

Further reader activities

1 Look at the text(s) included in the next unit of a course book which you are using, and see whether any of them activate vocabulary. If there are no activities designed to practise vocabulary and you feel that this would be worthwhile, design a speaking activity which will achieve this.

2 Find a text which contains a lexical set (approximately six items) that would be useful to your students. How would you teach the items? Consider the following:

a) Could the students predict the presence of this lexical area from the topic of the text?

b) Can the items be guessed from the context?

c) Are they so crucial to an understanding of the text that some need to be pre-taught?

Select one or more of the above approaches for presentation and then refer to the rest of this chapter for an idea that could be used for further practice of the set.

3 Find a text from a course book which includes an exercise on contextual guesswork and then ask your students to underline all the new items in the text. Consider the following:

a) Have the students underlined the target items selected by the writer?

b) Do the target items selected by the writer represent, in your opinion, the most useful of the new items?

c) Is the presence of other new words significant enough to interfere with the students' ability to guess the target items?

9 Teacher designed contexts and the use of the dictionary

Designing your own vocabulary activities has the great advantage that you can exercise complete control over the input. The other side of the coin is that it can be very time-consuming. For this reason, we have tried to include types of activity that can easily be reproduced for different lexical areas.

We have already discussed the use of dictionaries in a previous chapter, but we would like to add one word of warning about their use in the classroom. Despite being a valuable source of information, dictionaries are not perfect, and it is very unwise to make prior assumptions about the type of information included or the manner in which it is expressed. So, if you want to avoid setting your students a fruitless task which could undermine their confidence in you and the dictionary, we would recommend that you check all the dictionary entries relevant to the particular task before going into the classroom.

i) DEFINITIONS AND PICTURES (OALDCE)

Level: Advanced, although this type of activity can be adapted for most levels above elementary.

Suggested procedure: Select twelve lexical items from the dictionary that are all accompanied by a picture. The items should all be new to the students. Divide your class into paired A and B groups of six (if you have twenty-four students, for example, you will have two A groups and two B groups). Next, copy out the words with their dictionary definitions on a separate sheet of paper, giving six examples to each A group and six to each B group. Thus:

Group A

syr·inge /sɪˈrɪndʒ/ *n* kinds of device for drawing in liquid by suction and forcing it out again in a fine stream, used for washing out wounds, injecting liquids into the body, in spraying plants, etc: *a hypodermic* ∼; *a garden* ∼. □ *vt* [VP6A,15B] clean, inject liquid into, with a ∼; apply (liquid) with a ∼.

bat¹ /bæt/ *n* small mouse–like animal that flies at night and feeds on fruit and insects. ⇨ the illus at small.

≫→

125

fly·over /'flaɪəʊvə(r)/ *n* **1** (US = *overpass*) roadway, bridge, etc which crosses above another roadway, etc (as on a motorway).

span·ner /'spænə(r)/ *n* (US = *wrench*) tool for gripping and turning nuts on screws, bolts, etc. ⇨ the illus at tool. **throw a '∼ in/into the works,**

barb /bɑːb/ *n* back-turning or back-curving point of an arrow, spear, fish-hook, etc. **∼ed** *adj* having a ∼ or ∼s. **∼ed wire,** wire with short, sharp points, used for fences, etc: *∼ed wire entanglements,* for defensive purposes in war.

sling¹ /slɪŋ/ *n* [C] **1** band of material, length of rope, chain, etc looped round an object, eg a barrel, a broken arm, to support or lift it.

Group B

blink·ers /'blɪŋkəz/ *n pl* (US = *blinders*) leather squares to prevent a horse from seeing sideways. ⇨ the illus at **harness.**

scythe /saɪð/ *n* tool with a slightly curved blade on a long wooden pole with two short handles, for cutting long grass, grain, etc. ☐ *vt* [VP6A,15A] cut with a ∼.

'safetypin, pin bent with a guard at one end to protect and hold fast the point at the other end. ⇨ the illus at **safety.**

mit·ten /'mɪtn/ *n* **1** kind of glove covering four fingers together and the thumb separately. **2** covering for the back and palm of the hand only, leaving the thumb and fingers bare.

bon·net /'bɒnɪt/ *n* **1** protective cover of various sorts, eg over a chimney, or (US = *hood*) over the engine of a motor-car. ⇨ the illus at **motor.**

dam¹ /dæm/ *n* **1** barrier built to keep back water and raise its level (eg to form a reservoir, or for hydro-electric power). (Cf *barrage,* a barrier across a river, usu for irrigation purposes.)

Each group discusses their words and definitions in an attempt to reach agreement on their understanding of the items. It may seem strange to talk about discussing a 'definition', but dictionary definitions are not always very straightforward.

With a monolingual group this will probably involve agreeing upon a suitable mother-tongue equivalent. At this stage you should monitor the groups without confirming or rejecting any of their answers. When the students have finished, each member of group A tries to explain the meaning of his words to a member of group B, and vice versa. After each explanation both students look up the word with accompanying picture to see if they have arrived at the correct answer.

Comment: Many dictionaries include pictures to reinforce meaning but often they are grouped within semantic fields and do not appear on the same page as the dictionary entry. In such cases there will be a reference to the picture at the end of the definition. In our experience many students either fail to notice this reference or are unaware of its significance. This activity should help students become more aware of the use of visuals in the dictionary and also give them practice in defining and paraphrasing. We have already discussed this in chapter 5, and you may decide to teach relevant transactional language prior to this particular activity.

Students may also find in this activity that they are unable to understand some of the items from the dictionary definition alone. This may be the fault of the dictionary in not providing a very clear definition or explanation, but it is more likely to reveal the immense difficulty of the task that a dictionary undertakes. For many items it is just not possible to convey the meaning very satisfactorily by a handful of words and a single sentence example. Students should be made aware of these limitations and should recognise that dictionaries are not infallible.

ii)   WORDS EASILY CONFUSED: 'FALSE FRIENDS' *(LASDE)*

Level: Upper-intermediate, particularly for speakers of cognate languages e.g. Romance and Germanic languages.

Suggested procedure: Begin by explaining what a false cognate is, and illustrate the problem with one or two amusing examples that are relevant to your learners. (See ch. 1, exs. 1 and 2 for ideas.) Then produce a worksheet on the same lines as the one on the following page, (or use this one if applicable) containing appropriate lexis. Follow the procedure given on the student worksheet. Before asking students to do the final exercise, you may wish to conduct a feedback session to clarify any misunderstandings.

Comment: This particular exercise was designed for a mixed nationality class which was composed primarily of speakers of Romance languages. Clearly, you will need to select the items which cause most difficulty for your students. This type of activity is a useful way of highlighting the problem and bringing together items where student error is potentially very high.

127

Classroom activities

Be very careful with the words below. They may have different meanings from words which *look* the same in your own language. Look at the sentences below. For each sentence there are two different definitions of the words underlined. Only *one* definition is correct. Firstly, √ tick the answer you *think* is correct.

1 He's a *sympathetic* person.
   a) He's nice, fun to be with.
   b) He's very understanding e.g. you can tell him your problems.

2 She's very *sensible*.
   a) She's practical and doesn't do silly things.
   b) She's easily affected or upset by things people say to her.

3 He's a *sensitive* person.
   a) He's practical and doesn't do silly things.
   b) He's easily affected or upset by things people say to him.

4 She's a *confident* girl.
   a) She can keep secrets if you tell her them.
   b) She's sure of herself.

5 He's a *terrific* uncle.
   a) All the children love him.
   b) All the children are afraid of him.

6 He's a *famous* actor.
   a) Everybody knows who he is.
   b) He's great, a fantastic actor.

Now use your dictionary to check whether your answers are correct.

Fill the gaps using the words underlined above.
1 We saw a .... film yesterday – it had everything – love, excitement, adventure – we enjoyed every minute of it!
2 Don't mention her big ears, she's terribly .... about them.
3 It isn't very .... to go on holiday in England without an umbrella.
4 I wouldn't like to be ....; it must be boring to sign autographs and be nice to everyone all the time.
5 The doctor wasn't very .... when I showed him the cut on my leg; in fact, he said I was wasting his time!
6 Jenny won't pass her exam because she isn't .... in herself.

iii)   WORD BUILDING *(LASDE)*

Level: Intermediate.

Suggested procedure: Distribute the handout and tell the students to complete the table with the help of their dictionaries. The *LASDE* is particularly good for this lexical set as it provides simple but clear distinctions between a number of the items under the entry for 'thief'. You will probably need to clarify the difference between 'theft' and 'robbery', and 'steal' and 'rob'; in the case of the latter there are also the grammatical differences.

Practice: On completion of the first activity the students can work on the two texts with accompanying questions. These are designed to test the students' knowledge of the items as well as providing scope for free practice and lively discussion.

Comment: Course books often include word building tables of this kind, and sometimes include gap filling exercises to test the items. If there is a weakness in course book material it is usually the absence of relevant practice activities for the new vocabulary.

>>>→

Use your dictionary to complete the table below.

Criminal	Crime	Verb
e.g. a burglar a thief	e.g. burglary theft murder rape arson shoplifting pickpocketing	e.g. to burgle to mug to rob – to shoplift (rare) –

Now read the following case histories and discuss the questions below.

A. Joseph Simmons lived a life of crime for over twenty years. He stole cameras and electrical goods from busy department stores during the day, as well as taking money from innocent tourists in street markets and crowded shopping areas. At night he broke into numerous houses in West London where he stole anything from diamond rings to saucepans and cutlery. On several occasions he even used violence to obtain money from helpless old ladies in the street. At the moment he is in court for taking £2,000 from a small bank in East London. He was alone but carried a gun.

B. Brian Coleman was a shy boy who loved animals but found it very difficult to talk to other people or make friends. His father was a strong aggressive man who often drank too much and beat his son violently. Brian's mother had died when Brian was born. At the age of fourteen Brian set fire to his school in the middle of the night, when the building was empty and then ran away from home. He was caught and sent to a detention centre for young criminals where he spent two very unhappy years with stronger more violent boys. He was not allowed to keep any pets during this time. When he was released he met a fifteen-year-old girl and forced her to have sex with him. Now he is in court for this crime.

1 Name the crimes committed by both men.
2 List the crimes in order of seriousness.
3 What do you think will or should happen to each man?
4 What do you think each man would do if he were not sent to prison?

iv)   VERB PATTERNS *(OALDCE)*

Level: Intermediate upwards.

Suggested procedure: Show your students the table of verb patterns at the back of the dictionary and provide more examples to illustrate the patterns you intend to focus on. Then give the students the handout and ask them to complete the first exercise, using the dictionary to check their answers. If they are able to do this successfully they can move on to the second exercise on the handout.

Practice: For further practice see the role play on page 145.

Comment: This particular feature of the dictionary can be extremely daunting, and it certainly demands a very thorough and methodical approach on the part of the learner to fully reap the benefits. For this reason we have restricted the activity to verbs the students should already know, allowing them to focus entirely on the verb patterns (a very common source of student error). It is also important to reassure your students that they will not need to learn all the patterns. However, there will still be students who find this type of retrieval exercise boring and far too painstaking; do not be discouraged by this or make the mistake of bullying the students into repeating the exercise. You have alerted your students to an important, if complex, feature of the dictionary, and some students will derive enormous benefit from this knowledge.

STUDENT ACTIVITY

Which of the following verbs can you use to complete the sentence in the boxes below? Use your dictionary to check your answers and notice that there is more than one correct answer in some of the examples.

tell   advise   suggest   warn   insist   (VP = verb pattern)

1 VP 17

He The doctor		me the patient her	not	to stay to take to smoke	in bed. the pills.

2 VP 11

He		me him John	that	smoking was bad for my health.

»»→

3 VP 9

He The doctor		that	I go I should go I went	to bed.

4 VP 6C

She The nurse		going to bed.

5 VP 3A

She The nurse		on	him his	going to bed.

Report these statements made by the doctor using the verbs from the previous exercise:

e.g. 'I think you should give up smoking.'
The doctor advised me to give up smoking.

1 'Why don't you try giving up smoking?'
....

2 'If you don't stop smoking it'll get worse.'
....

3 'Take one pill three time a day.'
....

4 'You must rest for at least a week.'
....

5 'If I were you, I'd take a week off work.'
....

v) MEANING: ADJECTIVES DESCRIBING ACCOMMODATION
    (LASDE)

Level: Intermediate.

Suggested procedure: Put the students in pairs, and then give out the handout containing the retrieval activity and the exercise. While the students are working you should monitor the activities; the pronunciation may be a particular problem in one or two cases, and you may find it useful to pre-teach this.

Practice: Students can use the adjectives to describe:
   a) their classroom.
   b) their own bedrooms.
For further practice see the role play on page 149.

STUDENT ACTIVITY

Use your dictionary to look up the words below, decide if they are positive or negative, and give an explanation.

cosy gloomy damp spacious cramped draughty luxurious

Positive	Explanation	Negative	Explanation
e.g. spacious	lots of space		

Now complete the following sentences with one of the above adjectives.
1 The place where I stayed was so .... that I didn't have any room to store anything.
2 My new flat isn't very big but I like it because it's so ....
3 The problem with basement flats is that they can be very ....
4 It's one of the most .... houses I've ever seen; a bathroom for every bedroom, colour TV in every room, and a swimming pool on the roof.
5 My new flat isn't beautiful or very comfortable but it's very ....
6 My flat is so .... that it still feels cold when the central heating is on.
7 I think the flat is .... because I keep getting colds and there is a funny smell everywhere.

© 1986 Cambridge University Press

133

vi) PHONEMICS EXERCISE *(LDCE)*

Level: Lower-intermediate though could be adapted to suit any level.

Suggested procedure: Teach/revise the sounds and corresponding phonemic symbols (in this case /ʌ/, /uː/, /əʊ/, /ɒ/) and then select a
number of items which share certain spelling patterns but differ in
pronunciation. It is a good idea to include some items already known
to the students to give them confidence, plus items that are commonly
mispronounced, and several new items with unpredictable pronunciation. Tell the students to check the meaning of any new items and
use the phonemic transcription in their dictionaries to place the items
in the correct column.

cough   blood   chew   couple   brooch   sew   hot   choose   lose
hotel   move   lost   holiday   oven   lonely   other

/ʌ/	/uː/	/əʊ/	/ɒ/
e.g. son	e.g. soon	e.g. so	e.g. soft

After checking the answers on the blackboard you should also check
that students understand the new lexical items; in this case we would
anticipate that 'cough', 'brooch', 'oven', 'chew', and 'sew' may be
new to some or all of the group.

Practice: Divide the class into pairs and ask them to read the following
text. Their task is to identify the number of times that each sound
appears.

Last year I went on holiday on my own. I spent ten days in Venice
followed by one week in Rome. In Venice it was a disaster. It was
so hot my hotel room was like an oven, I had a terrible cough
and sore throat for a week, I lost my camera, and I was lonely.
When I moved on to Rome it was different. I soon met a couple
of other people from Germany who spoke English, and I had a
great time with them.

Comment: Linking phonemics and phonology teaching to the dictionary
in this way should help to convince students that the sound/spelling
irregularities in English need not be an insurmountable obstacle to
good pronunciation.

vii) JUMBLED SENTENCES: PARTIAL SYNONYMS

Level: Intermediate.

Suggested procedure: Using the first exercise from the handout ask the students to match sentences from the left hand column with their logical counterpart in the right hand column; they can do this individually or in pairs. We are assuming that 'employ' and 'dismiss' will already be known to some of the students, which leaves them with the relatively simple task of finding the remaining two answers; their dictionaries will confirm whether they are right or not. The students will probably be able to deduce the difference between 'dismiss' and 'make somebody redundant' but this needs to be clarified before moving on.

The second exercise is almost identical so the students should realise that the italicised items are synonyms of the items contained in the first section; shared knowledge, dictionaries, and a process of elimination should enable them to complete the task.

When the students have finished you will need to clarify the possible syntactic variations with 'take on' and 'lay off', and the stylistic variation with some of the items. You may also wish to add the noun 'resignation' plus the use of 'sack' as a noun i.e. to give somebody the sack.

Practice: Put the students into small groups and ask them to discuss the situations listed at the end of the handout. Encourage them to use the vocabulary from the activity before. At the end, conduct a feedback session to compare group answers; this could possibly be done on the blackboard.

Comment: This is an area of vocabulary where there are a number of partially synonymous items. We are exploiting this fact by using known items to direct students towards the meaning of unknown items. The lexis included in this activity clearly makes it more suitable for adult groups.

>>>→

Classroom activities

Using the grid below, match the numbers on the left with the letters on the right to form four logical sentences.

1 The company has decided to *employ* ten more workers	A because of the economic recession.
2 The company has decided to *dismiss* ten workers	B because they are going to open a new factory.
3 The company has decided to *make* ten workers *redundant*	C because of the poor safety regulations.
4 Ten workers have decided to *resign*	D because they were consistently late for work.

Now do the same for the grid below.

1 The company has decided to *sack* ten more workers	A because of the poor safety regulations.
2 The company has decided to *lay off* ten more workers	B because they are going to open a new factory.
3 Ten workers have *handed in* their *notice*	C because they were consistently late for work.
4 The company has decided to *take on* ten more workers	D because of the economic recession.

Now discuss the following questions in small groups.
1 Can you think of three reasons why you would resign from your present job?
2 If you had to make redundancies, how would you decide which workers to make redundant? (e.g. those employed the shortest time in the company; the laziest workers; workers near the age of retirement?)
3 You are the boss of a company that sells breakfast cereals to supermarkets. You discover that one of your salesmen has been giving part of his commission to one of the supermarket managers; in return the manager displays your product in a favourable position in the shop. What action would you take?

© 1986 Cambridge University Press

viii) LEXICAL CONNECTIVES

Level: Intermediate upwards.

Suggested procedure: Everything you need for this activity is contained in the student worksheet, so your main task is in ensuring that the students have clearly understood each section of the worksheet before going on to the next phase.

Comment: The activity is designed to teach 'although', 'though' and 'even though', but also to show the value of lexical connectives in deducing the meaning of unknown items in a text.

STUDENT ACTIVITY

1 Look at this sentence.

Although he didn't have much money, he bought her a lovely present.

Does it mean the same as (a) or (b) below?
a) He bought her a lovely present because he didn't have much money.
b) He didn't have much money, but he bought her a lovely present.

(q) :*ɹǝʍsu∀*

| although
even though
though | $\rightarrow$ are all adverbs which link or connect two *contrasting* ideas. |

Look again at the example. The fact that he bought her a lovely present is rather *surprising* or *unexpected*, because we know that he didn't have much money.

There is very little difference in meaning between 'although', 'even though' and 'though'. 'Although' is a little more formal, and common in writing. With 'even though', 'even' adds emphasis and surprise.

Notice that you are using these connectives to join two clauses.

| although
even though
though | x, | y. | (or) | y, | although
even though
though | x. |

≫→

137

2 Which of the sentences below use 'although', 'even though' and 'though' correctly?
   a) We enjoyed our holiday, even though the weather was terrible.
   b) We hated the boat trip though the sea wasn't calm.
   c) Spain was lovely even though the weather was really nice.
   d) Although I don't like ice-cream, I can eat it if I have to.
   In the sentences that *aren't* correct which connectives should you use?

   Answers: (a) and (d) are right, (b) and (c) are incorrect. In (b) and (c) it would be acceptable to say 'and', or 'because'.

   Now that you understand these connectives, complete these sentences in your own words.
   a) Even though I didn't enjoy the film ....
   b) I didn't like John, though ....
   c) Although Shakespeare's plays are difficult to read, ...
   d) He looked very ill though ....

3 Now use your knowledge of the connectives to guess the meaning of *other* words you don't know; remember that 'although', 'even though' and 'though' link contrasting ideas.
   The words underlined below are all *colloquial*. What do you think they mean?
   ((d) is an idiom.)
   a) He failed his exam even though he *swotted* hard for it before.
   b) He *flunked* the test even though he was the cleverest in the class.
   c) Richard managed to understand the maths lesson, though he is a bit *dim*.
   d) Although his teacher told him *to pull his socks up*, he continued to be a lazy student.
   Now use your dictionary to check if your answers were correct.

© 1986 Cambridge University Press

ix) ADJECTIVE–NOUN COMBINATIONS: 'OPPOSITES'

Level: Upper-intermediate, though the type of activity could be adapted for intermediate upwards.
Suggested items:

1	2	3	4
left	– right	a right answer	– a wrong answer
married	– single	a single ticket	– a return ticket
wet	– dry	dry wine	– sweet wine
soft	– hard	a hard job	– an easy job
weak	– strong	a strong smell	– a faint smell
smooth	– rough	a rough sea	– a calm sea
heavy	– light	a light colour	– a dark colour
hot	– cold	a cold person	– a warm person
low	– high	a high voice	– a deep voice

Suggested procedure: Prepare small prompt cards for each of the items in the third column above:

e.g. | a right answer | | a single ticket | etc.

In the activity above, there are ten examples, so if you have a class of nine, give them one prompt card each and keep the first prompt card to demonstrate the activity. (For larger classes, divide the students into groups of nine and photocopy enough prompt cards for everyone.)

You can adapt this activity to suit the number of students in your class quite easily. Begin by asking the class:

Teacher: What's the opposite of left?
Students: Right.

Teacher shows prompt | a right answer |

Teacher: Ah, but what's the opposite of a right *answer*?
At this point some students may be able to supply the answer ('a wrong answer') and thus teach the rest of the group; if not, supply the answer yourself. Go back and repeat the exchange.

Proceed to the next example. When a student hears the adjective on his card, he has to say the third line of dialogue. Frequent recapping in this activity will ensure considerable controlled practice for the students. This is also a useful opportunity to focus on stress shift (e.g. here, the stress in lines 1 and 2 is on the adjective, but in the third line falls on 'answer' – the new information focus). At the end, the 'opposites' should be written on the blackboard and copied by the students into their notebooks.

Practice: Put the students in pairs and give them two or three adjectives each. Ask them to devise prompt questions using these adjectives:

e.g. Is your brother *rich*?
Did you buy a *single* ticket?
Would you like *dry* wine?

One pair then asks another a question which they answer using an 'opposite':

e.g. Pair A: Is your neighbour rich?
Pair B: No, he's poor.
Pair A: Did you buy a single ticket?
Pair B: No, we bought a return ticket.

Comment: Some of the examples above are collocations and this shows that it is occasionally possible to link them thematically. In the case of food, there are several useful ones in the exercise above, and one could also include tough/tender; sweet/savoury; sweet/sour; strong/mild; strong/weak. In this case, it is not difficult to provide communicative practice through a restaurant role play. Divide the class into groups of customers with a waiter to each table. Provide them with menus and ask them to order; then give customers prompt cards describing a problem ('You asked for sweet wine, but this wine isn't sweet') and encourage them to complain politely to the waiter.

x) NON-GRADABLE ADJECTIVES: 'EXTREMES' *(LDCE)*

Level: Advanced, but with simpler lexis could be used at lower levels.

Suggested procedure: Illustrate the concept of 'non-gradable' or 'extreme' adjectives using the scale on the worksheet. Ask the students to use their dictionaries and shared knowledge to check the meaning and pronunciation of the extreme adjectives, and to do the exercise below. Discuss whether these adjectives are applicable to other nouns (e.g. 'hideous' could be used for a building, a town centre, a person, an animal, etc.).

Practice: When you are going over the exercise as a group, demonstrate an appropriate intonation pattern for the response. Students can then test each other in pairs; only one student in the pair can look at the worksheet and he gives the stimulus to his partner i.e.

Student A: Their dog's rather ugly, isn't it?

Student B: Ugly? It's absolutely hideous!

For a game to reinforce these adjectives, see page 164.

Comment: This could easily be adapted for a lower level by changing the extreme adjectives e.g. good/fantastic; big/enormous.

Look at these: rather
                   very | cold *but* absolutely freezing
                   quite |

Freezing is at the end of extreme on a scale of coldness.

rather cold	cold	very cold	freezing

You can say that something is 'absolutely' freezing, but you can't say that it is 'very freezing'.

Change the following sentences by supplying the appropriate 'extreme' adjective from the list below:

priceless	hilarious	ghastly
invaluable	gorgeous	colossal
unique	outrageous	minute
terrifying	revolting	hideous

1 A: It must have been unpleasant to see everyone around you on the boat being sick.
     B: Unpleasant? It was absolutely revolting!
2 Their dog's rather ugly, isn't it?
3 They give very small portions in that restaurant, don't they?
4 Did you think he was funny?
5 It's a valuable painting, isn't it?
6 Your guide book is useful, isn't it?
7 She's beautiful, isn't she?
8 He's got a big library, hasn't he?
9 You've had a bad day, then?
10 This coin is rare, isn't it?
11 His behaviour is rather offensive, don't you think?
12 It was a frightening experience, wasn't it?

xi) WORD BUILDING

Level: Upper-intermediate upwards.

Suggested procedure: Distribute copies of the worksheet (which is self-explanatory) and ask the students to fill in the grid. Remind them that adjectives relating to nationalities must start with capital letters. They may wish to use dictionaries to check their answers and it would be useful to conduct a feedback session to clarify any difficulties before the students move onto the gap fill exercise. Point out to the students that in the last column there is a restricted number of generative examples and these are generally common descriptive adjectives.

This activity could lead to oral practice and allow the students to generate their own examples if you give them pictures of people (also famous people) to describe e.g. Paul Newman is shortish, sixtyish and with greyish hair.

STUDENT ACTIVITY

The suffix '+ish' has several different meanings.

1 *Denoting nationality*	e.g. Swedish = from Sweden.
2 *Approximately:* with times, numbers (informal)	e.g. at sixish = at about six o'clock; fiftyish = about fifty.
3 *Somewhat, rather, tending towards* (informal)	e.g. fattish = tending to be fat; greenish = a vague green colour.
4 *Typical of, in the manner of* (often pejorative)	e.g. foolish = like a fool, typical of a fool.

Now look at the list below and divide the adjectives into the four categories, according to the meaning of '+ish' in each case.

spanish childish snobbish irish tallish flemish boyish devilish
finnish six-thirtyish youngish latish sixtyish blackish roundish

nationality	*typical of, in the manner of*	*approximately*	*somewhat, tending towards*

Complete the sentences using a word from the list above.
1 He's just retired from work so he must be ....
2 How would I describe her? Well, she's got a .... face, and she's .... – can't be more than 20 years old.
3 You wouldn't think he was an adult – his behaviour is so ....
4 She lives in Belgium so perhaps she speaks ....
5 I'll see you in front of the theatre – shall we say ....?
6 He's so .... that he won't even talk to anyone he thinks is inferior.

© 1986 Cambridge University Press

Further reader activities

1 Design a worksheet to teach one of the following:
   a) 'because of' versus 'in spite of'
   b) 'although' versus 'whereas'
   c) 'if', 'unless' and 'otherwise'
   Use the activity on page 137 as an example and provide sentences
   for students to guess the meaning of unknown words.
2 Design a word building chart similar to the one on page 130 for
   one of the following:
   a) political vocabulary
   b) countries and nationalities
   c) sciences
   d) academic study
3 If your students speak a cognate language, devise a worksheet to highlight false friends based on the activity on page 128.
4 Devise a sound/spelling activity similar to the one on page 134 to
   practise a sound which presents particular difficulties for your students.

10 Speaking activities

Most readers will be familiar with narrative and role play as they are regularly used in the classroom for further practice of important structures and functions/notions in the syllabus. Vocabulary teaching in these activities is usually relegated to second place, the choice of target lexis being determined by the topic which incorporates the particular structure or function. Unfortunately, this can result in students learning a lot of vocabulary which serves a classroom need, but has little intrinsic value.

We feel sure that the suggestions in this section will still provide useful practice for a wide variety of structures and functions; we have simply changed the emphasis by making vocabulary the first priority. In each case, we have drawn on our classroom experience, and included speaking activities which we hope will provide the kind of interesting and generative practice so often neglected in many courses.

10.1 Role play

i) AIRPORT ENQUIRIES (see text on p. 116 for presentation of vocabulary)

Level: Intermediate.
Suggested procedure: In this activity two students operate the Information Desk at an airport, and the remaining students make a variety of travel enquiries. In addition to the vocabulary already presented you will also need to pre-teach the phrases 'schedule'/'due to arrive at...'

Start by giving the two students a series of cards, each one containing information about flight arrivals and departures:
e.g. Flight: BA429 from Munich
     Scheduled arrival: 14.40
     Time now: 15.40
     Information: Fog. One hour delay. Just landed.
Now send both students out of the room to study their information. Give the remaining students a role card with a specific enquiry e.g. 'You are meeting your mother who is flying from Munich. The plane was due to land at 2.40 p.m. It's now 3.40 p.m. What has happened?'

You can now invite the two students back into the room, seat them at opposite ends of the room, and ask the other students to take it in turns to get up and make their enquiry. A more interesting variation, however, is to invite the students to make their enquiries before the preceding student has finished. The effect of this is to put more pressure on the students, to introduce a wider range of functions, and to make the activity more fun. The result is often enjoyable chaos, which can be repeated several times by giving each student a new card.

Comment: This is the type of situation where appropriate lexis can compensate for grammatical or functional inadequacy. The student interaction is fairly brief but quite demanding, and we would be surprised if the students were able to handle the situation without running into one or two problems; much will depend, of course, on the nature of the information on their role cards. However, we would hope that a knowledge of the relevant vocabulary would be sufficient for them to achieve their aim.

ii) VERB PATTERNS (see p. 131)

Level: Intermediate.

Suggested procedure: For this activity four members of the class are 'doctors' and the remainder 'patients'. Start by giving each 'patient' a role card with a complaint written on it e.g. you can't sleep / you're putting on weight / you've got a pain in your back', etc. Then allow them two or three minutes to think about their complaint and develop the details i.e. when? why? how? how long? While they are thinking about this you instruct the four students acting as doctors that they must listen to the patients' complaints and then offer advice, suggestions, orders, or instructions for each patient. Each doctor should then be seated in a different part of the classroom.

When the patients are ready they must take it in turns to consult the doctors. Each patient must talk to each of the four doctors and make a note of the advice given to them, as do the doctors. At the end of the activity the patients regroup into fours (the doctors forming a separate group). In this next phase each patient describes his complaint and the different advice given by the four doctors. The group must then decide who gave the best advice; doctors do likewise. Each student will now be using reported speech and they could be encouraged to use the verbs presented earlier i.e. advise, suggest, tell, warn, insist, selecting in each case the verb that corresponds in meaning to the doctor's actual words.

Comment: The amount of information you include on the role cards, and the extent to which you guide the students towards the target verbs, will obviously affect the degree of control you exercise over the students' language. At the preparation stage, therefore, you should decide exactly how much freedom you wish to allow your students and set up the role play accordingly. If you feel that the doctor/patient situation is not appropriate for your students, you could easily transfer the idea and target vocabulary to a different context e.g. advice/ suggestions/warnings on examinations to take, careers to follow, places to go on holiday, etc.

iii) SHOP ROLE PLAY

Level: Advanced.

Suggested procedure: Teach all the items in the visual and give students some controlled practice. Go on to discuss what they are used for and clarify any vocabulary necessary e.g. to undo, to unscrew, a nail, a bolt, etc. Divide the class into groups of about eight students, appointing two of the students as shopkeepers. Explain that one of them has a hardware shop and the other a second hand shop. Give them each their role card, and ask them to leave the room while they read through and absorb their information. Explain to the rest of the students that both shops are having a closing-down sale and that they are going to buy items in the shops. They are all in a hurry to buy and to find out which shop will give them the best bargain for their purchase. Once they have decided where to buy, they should make a note of it and the price. Give each student a card with their intended purchase:

e.g.

a spanner (any kind)	a saw – you want to do some carpentry at home

and also tell them that they are amnesiacs: they can't remember the word on the cards so have to describe the object or its use to the shopkeeper. Give this piece of information to the shopkeepers too, and tell them to remind the customers what the name of the object is:

e.g. Customer: I want one of those things you use for cutting wire.
　　 Shopkeeper: Oh, you want a pair of pliers.

Ask the shopkeepers to return and sit them in different parts of the room. Ask two students to go and buy something from each shop and almost immediately send another pair to interrupt and get the ball rolling. Once students have been to both shops and made their decision they should come to the teacher for another prompt card and buy something else.

Comment: Apart from the target vocabulary, there is a wide range of language practice here. Shopkeepers will have to delay customers, ask

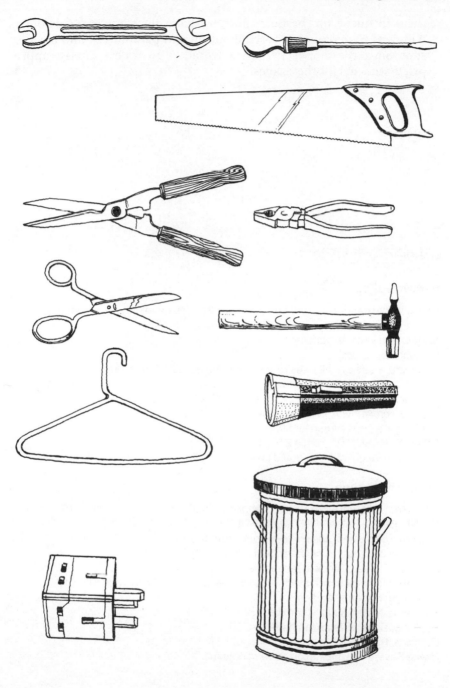

them to queue up, be quiet and persuade them to buy. Customers will need to describe (i.e. use definition and paraphrase) and to interrupt. Since the shopkeepers have to talk a great deal, choose appropriate students for these roles.

Hardware shop

You sell *coat hangers* in bunches of five for £1. You have only got wooden ones.
You've run out of *adaptors*. (They'll be here on . . .?)
Shears with wooden handles £8.50.
You don't sell *scissors*.
Spanners: You have all sizes ranging in price from £1.50–£6.00.
You've only got very small *saws* in stock £1.50.
Hammers: wooden handles £2.50, plastic £3.80.
You sell *screwdrivers* in packs of five (different sizes) £3.50.
You've got a child's *torch* for 80p.
Dustbins: large, plastic ones £10, metal £7.50.
Pliers: You've got one pair you'd love to sell at £8.

Second hand shop

You've got different types of *coat hangers* (plastic, wooden, wire) all at 10p each.
You've got one (rather dirty) *adaptor* £1.20.
You have one pair of *shears* with plastic handles £4.
Your *scissors* aren't very sharp. Sell them at 60p if you can.
Spanners: none in stock at the moment.
You've got a large *saw* in stock – for two people to cut down trees with £18.
Hammers: wooden handles only £2.
You sell only very small *screwdrivers* at 15p.
You've got a large *torch* (no batteries) £3.
Dustbins: Rather old, the one you've got £2?
Pliers: Several, all at £2.50 in good condition.

© 1986 Cambridge University Press

iv) COMPLAINING (see p. 133 for presentation)

Level: Intermediate.

Suggested procedure: Divide the class in half and send one group out of the classroom for two minutes. Explain to the remainder that they are guests in a hotel but are extremely unhappy with the room they have been given. Tell them to think about their complaint and encourage them to incorporate some of the negative vocabulary from the exercise on page 133. While they are preparing their complaint you can join the other group who will play the part of the hotel receptionist. Their job is to please the guests and they should be encouraged to employ the positive vocabulary from the exercise in order to reassure the unhappy guests. However, it is more interesting if you throw in a few suggestions to complicate the situation e.g. you have a room available which isn't damp, draughty, gloomy or cramped, but it is more expensive or rather noisy as it overlooks the main road.

Bring the students back into the classroom, put one receptionist with either one or two guests and get them to act out the situation.

Comment: Hotel situations are relevant for many foreign learners of English and they are also very versatile i.e. they can be manipulated for vocabulary practice in a wide range of lexical areas.

10.2 Narrative

i) NARRATIVE THROUGH VISUALS

Level: Any level.

Suggested procedure: Select a group of items you wish to practise/revise and draw them on small pieces of card (one item per card). Divide the class into small groups, and give each group six cards. Make sure they do not show their pictures to the other groups. Each group must then construct a narrative that will include all the items they have been given e.g:

I have all my old clothes in a *suitcase* and yesterday I decided that I wanted to wear an old grey scarf and black pair of *gloves* that were in the suitcase. Unfortunately the suitcase was locked and I couldn't find the *key*; so, I got a *knife* from the kitchen and tried to break the lock. I couldn't but I cut my finger and there was blood all over my mother's best carpet. I ran to the bathroom turned on the *tap*, and washed off all the blood. I looked in the bathroom cupboard for some plasters but couldn't find any. Then I noticed the key to my suitcase under some towels. Feeling better I went back to my room and opened the suitcase. It was empty except for a *pair of scissors*, some suntan lotion and some plasters.

When they have finished each group reads their story to the rest of the class, and the students have to guess what pictures each group was given.

Comment: This activity can be easier or more difficult not only by the choice of items but also by the distribution of the cards. With advanced classes it is more challenging and often more fun to give each group a very disparate set of items that will demand a fairly complex or ingenious narrative in order to thread them together.

ii) NARRATIVE: PICTURE COMPOSITION

Picture stories are a valuable and widely used source of language practice material, and are commonly exploited either to provide controlled practice of structures, vocabulary and functional exponents, or to act as a stimulus for the communicative skill of narrating. It is not within the scope of this book to discuss how picture stories should and can be exploited generally: we are restricting ourselves here to a list of suggestions as to how the area of vocabulary can be approached with this type of material. The ideas suggested below are not necessarily all applicable to the picture story 'Jogging', but we suggest that next time you decide to use this type of material with a class, you check the suggestions to see if any of them are particularly relevant.

In addition to the obvious possibilities of pre-teaching the necessary vocabulary or feeding it in as students work through the story, we suggest the following.

Suggestions

– Tell the students that they are going to look at a picture story about a fat man who goes jogging and has a lot of problems. Ask them to form groups or pairs and predict the items which are likely to occur. At this stage they may wish to ask you how to say certain things in English. Write their suggestions on the blackboard. At the end, give them the pictures so that they can check which items would be needed.

– Split the class into two groups. Ask one group to predict the vocabulary as above, and ask the other group to look at the pictures and decide which vocabulary is relevant to telling the story. At the end, let the groups compare answers.

– Allow the students to see the *last* picture in the sequence and ask them to predict some of the vocabulary from the previous pictures. Then show them the pictures so that they can check their predictions.

– Show all the students the picture story and ask them to work through it in pairs, deciding which items they will need to use when telling the story and which items they cannot express in English. They can use paraphrase, definition or the pictures themselves to ask about new items.

– The same activity as above, but allow students to use bilingual dictionaries to find out. Conduct a feedback session to check the items.

– Give the students a series of pairs of items and a relevant picture number. Ask them to decide which of the two items they would need to use and which would be less appropriate or useful:
   e.g. Picture 5 – 'to fall down' or 'to fall over'.
   　　　Picture 8 – 'damp' or 'wet'.
   They should put the 'correct' item in a sentence.

– Write six to eight relevant (and probably unknown) items on the blackboard and show the students the pictures. Ask them to use their dictionaries to check the meaning and to decide *where* in the story each item would be used.

– With higher level students, give them a series of simple items of vocabulary and ask them to 'brainstorm' (i.e. use their shared knowledge) to find another way of expressing the idea:
   e.g. to laugh – to kill yourself laughing / to scream with laughter
   　　　to get very wet – to get soaked
   This simply provides a starting point and is a useful way of finding out what your students already know.

– Give the students a series of items and ask them to decide which of the items are *essential* for telling the story. They may need to use dictionaries to check the meaning first:
   e.g. 1 'running shoes' (not essential)
   　　　2 'to trip over' or 'to fall over' (one or the other essential)
   　　　3 'to tap someone on the shoulder' (not essential)
   　　　4 'a lead' or 'a leash' (not essential – 'he tripped over the dog' is perfectly acceptable; (this may require some explanation)
   　　　5 'to bite someone' or 'to attack someone' (essential)

– Give the students a written version of the story at the same time as

151

(from *Storylines*)

they see the pictures. Underline any key items you wish to highlight and ask them to deduce the meaning from the text and pictures:

e.g. 'As he came round the corner, he didn't see the dog and he *tripped over* it and hurt himself.'

(See p. 106 for a lengthier example of this.)

— Pre-teach or check appropriate connectives (e.g. because, just as, as soon as, so). Tell the students to decide where in the story they could be used.
— Before using the pictures, deal with word building and grammatical problems:

e.g. to jog, (to go) jogging; to put, to get, to hurt, to run, to bite, (all irregular).

This picture story is from *Storylines* (Fletcher and Birt, 1983) which includes practice activities such as gap filling, guided dialogue, role play and written consolidation.

iii) CO-OPERATIVE STORY TELLING

A woman was sitting in a café drinking tea one afternoon
(*describe the woman*)

Suddenly a man ran into the restaurant and shouted her name
(*what was her name?*)
(*describe the man*)

She looked frightened and went quickly to her bag for . . .
(*what did she want from her bag?*)

The man rushed up to her and hit her in the face.
(*how did she feel?*)
(*how did he feel?*)

(*what happened next?*)

Level: Lower-intermediate upwards.
Suggested procedure: Ask students to work in pairs for this activity. Explain that they are going to fill in the details of a story.
Write the first line of the story on the blackboard:

A woman was sitting . . .

Tell the pairs to describe the woman. (All instructions in brackets are for the students.) Ask them to make brief notes (e.g. tall / beautiful face / long black hair, etc.). It is useful to set a time limit for this. Continue with the next line of the story, writing it on the blackboard and giving the students their next instruction, and so on to the end.

Now ask each student to find a new partner and tell him his version of the story. Finally, ask one or two students to tell their story to the group.

Comment: This is based on the co-operative story telling activity in *Once Upon a Time* (Morgan and Rinvolucri, 1983), where you will find many excellent uses of narrative. The vocabulary revised here would cover physical descriptions, objects and emotions.

iv) MIME STORIES

Level: Any level.

Suggested procedure: Tell your students to watch you carefully and write down everything you do; they must not say anything while they are watching. You then perform a short mime of having a bath. When you have finished, put the students into pairs. Their task is to describe your mime to each other, adding details and correcting each other as they proceed. After a group feedback session to establish the most accurate record of the mime and clarify any lexical problems, the students can take it in turns to perform a short mime of their own.

This particular mime provides practice of multi-word verbs, including turn on/off (the tap), get into/out of (the bath), put on / take off (your clothes), sit down, hang up, etc. It can also be very amusing. A further example for multi-word verbs is 'tidying a room' e.g. tidy up, hang up, throw away, put away, take out, etc. The procedure is the same.

Comment: Mime stories can be exploited for further practice of a wide variety of lexical items, and they are also popular with a wide range of age groups.

10.3 Processes, priorities and appropriacy

i) PROCESSES

> *Life cycle*
>
> You get married.
> You fall in love with someone.
> You get to know someone.
> You have a baby.
> You go out with someone.
> You get divorced.
> You get engaged.

Level: Mid-intermediate.

Suggested procedure: The sentences above should be written on the blackboard in random order. At this stage, tell the students not to write down the sentences, but to use their dictionaries or shared knowledge to clarify the meaning and pronunciation of any items which are new or only partially known. You will probably need to check understanding, particularly with the use of 'get' and the meaning of 'have' in 'to have a baby'; the prepositions may also require some attention. Some teachers may wish to include some controlled practice at this stage.

Practice: Next, put the students in pairs and ask them to discuss the 'correct' order for these activities. When a pair have finished, ask them to find another pair and compare answers. Finally, ask one pair to tell the class the order they arrived at.

Now ask the students whether there are any variations to this order; whether, for example, they know of people whose life did not conform in the usual style, or whether they know about any variations in different cultures. Ask them to discuss this in small groups.

Comment: The area of vocabulary in this example contains problems of form rather than concept for most learners. The activity gives the students considerable oral practice, and at the same time allows the teacher to check that students have understood the items. It often works best when there are a variety of ways of ordering the same set; this gives the students the opportunity to discuss the process and draw on a wider range of vocabulary than that which is contained in the exercise. The initial check on meaning can be either learner-centred or teacher-centred. It is inadvisable with this type of activity to give the sentences on a handout at the beginning; if you do, the students may simply write numbers next to the sentences or point to them, which defeats the object of practice! It would also be worthwhile pre-teaching or pre-checking certain items of transactional language:

e.g. I think the first thing is ...   First of all you ...
     I think Y comes │ before │ X.   Then you ...
                     │ after │   After that you ...
     I think you Y │ before │ you X.
                   │ after │

Processes: some further suggestions

The sets of items below all have a suggested level next to them, however, the particular items chosen within a set could be made more or less sophisticated according to the group. Some sets are clearly suitable for certain groups of people; students who may be interested in business, scientific or technical English will find some of them very relevant. Some activities are more 'controversial' than others; in other words, there is a greater chance of variations on a standard order in some sets than in others.

1 *Daily routines* (elementary/lower-intermediate)
put on your clothes / get up / wake up / take off your pyjamas / go to the bathroom / clean your teeth / have breakfast / have a shower (wash, bath, shave)

2 *Being ill – having flu* (lower-intermediate)
you feel sick or dizzy / your body aches / you feel better / you stay in bed / you have a headache / you feel very tired / you call the doctor / you take aspirins / you get up

3 *Driving a car* (upper-intermediate)
turn the steering wheel / put the key in the ignition / use the indicator / look in the rear view mirror / get into the driving seat / put your foot on the clutch / adjust the rear view mirror / unlock the door / let the handbrake off / start the car / put the car in first gear / pull out
(This process often causes considerable argument.)

4 *Things you do in an exam* (upper-intermediate)
get up / go over your answers carefully / make up the answers you don't know / read through the questions / put your pen down / cross out anything which is wrong / note down your ideas roughly / try to make out what the questions mean / pick up your pen / write the essays out neatly.

5 *Releasing a record* (upper-intermediate/advanced)
write the lyrics / find the performers / launch a publicity campaign / compose the music / release the record / record the album / design the record sleeve / raise the capital / approach a recording company / edit the album

You may also wish to devise sets on the following topics:
Renting a flat, making a purchase, changing a plug, using an electrical gadget, making a dish or hot drink, being arrested, being tried, making a phone call, deciding on the order of dishes in a meal.
If your students are not particularly interested in very culture-bound content, you can make the topics above relevant to their own environment.

ii) PRIORITIES

The procedure for teaching and practising vocabulary through 'priorities' (see below) is much the same as the procedure we have suggested for 'Processes'. There are many splendid and extremely generative examples of sets of priorities in *Discussions that Work* (Penny Ur, 1981). Here is one of our own examples.

Priorities: contents of a suitcase

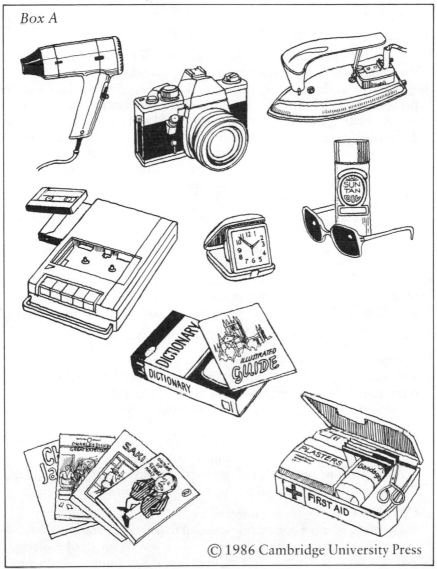

Box A

© 1986 Cambridge University Press

> *Box B*
>
> A *two month* stay in . . .
> a) an English-speaking country where you are going to attend a language school and stay in a student hostel
> b) a variety of hotels on a seaside holiday
> c) a holiday campsite abroad
> d) a foreign country where you will be working for a company full-time

Level: Lower-intermediate, could be adapted for any level, as long as the students have some knowledge of comparatives.

Suggested procedure: Look again at the suggested procedure for the process on page 155 as it is applicable here. Hand out a copy of box A, write the vocabulary for it on the blackboard and clarify any difficulties of meaning and pronunciation. Explain to the students that they are going abroad for two months, and while packing their suitcases they find they only have room for four out of the ten items on the list. They will not have any extra money to buy the remaining items when they go abroad. Put the students in pairs or small groups and ask them to take the situations in box B and come to an agreement as to which four items they will take in each instance. Once they have decided, they can pair up with another group and thrash out their arguments again until they reach a common decision.

Comment: Again, students will be able to have a considerable amount of oral practice of the target items. This particular exercise may also be a useful vehicle for revising suggestions and accepting and rejecting them, and 'going to' to express intention.

Priorities: further suggestions

1 *The bathroom shelf* (advanced, if using all the vocabulary suggested, but teachers could restrict the items for lower levels).

Using the situations in box B above, which *eight* items would they put in their suitcases?

talc/toothbrush/toothpaste/soap/flannel/mouthwash/sponge/
nailbrush/hairbrush/comb/shampoo/conditioner/deodorant/
razor/perfume or eau de cologne/bath or shower gel/shaving foam/
antiseptic/body cream/cotton wool/plasters/aspirins

2 *Giving up smoking* (upper-intermediate)

Put in order of most important or useful to least important or useful:
give up smoking with a friend / stay away from smoky places / throw away cigarettes and lighter / get rid of your ashtrays / put

aside the money you save / take up a new hobby / chew gum / eat sweets / tell all your friends you are giving up

3 *Qualities required for a job* (intermediate)
   Put qualities in order of importance for the jobs given:
   Qualities: patient / friendly / hard-working / dedicated / studious / responsible / imaginative / tactful / flexible
   Jobs: doctor / receptionist / actor / diplomat

Look back also at the text 'Holidays go to the top of the perks list' on page 120, for an example of a set of priorities linked to a text; the gadgets illustrated on page 78 could also be exploited here: which items are dispensable or indispensable in the house or flat where you live?

iii) APPROPRIACY

These exercises provide semi-controlled practice of vocabulary items and they can be done in groups or pairs. Students are asked in each case to discuss the suitability or appropriacy of items in a variety of contexts. This can be a useful way of bringing disparate items together e.g.

Containers
Level: Intermediate.
Suggested procedure: Begin by teaching the items of vocabulary listed in box A (i.e. tube, bag, etc.) either through realia or using the visuals in the exercise. Then ask the students to look at the items in box B and name one container in each case which is normally used for these goods e.g. washing-up liquid is usually sold in plastic bottles.

   Now put the students into pairs or groups and tell them to discuss each product in turn to find the maximum possible number of ways of packing it. They should consider the advantages and disadvantages in each case:
   e.g. *Yoghurt:* usually sold in *tubs*, could be packed in *bottles* (but may be difficult to get it out), great in a *tube* (you could eat it discreetly on a bus, for example), would last a long time in a *can*, not very easy to carry in a *plastic bag*, etc.
Comment: It is important to plan in advance how to give maximum practice in the target items. In the case of the 'containers' vocabulary, you need to ask the students to discuss the *goods* in turn. (If you ask them to take each container in turn, then inevitably students will practise the 'goods' vocabulary instead.)

Containers

Box A			
tube	bag	bottle	jar
can	tub	packet	sachet

Box B

1. washing-up liquid
2. yoghurt
3. perfume
4. beans (cooked)
5. glue
6. aspirins
7. fresh cream
8. coca cola

Appropriacy: further suggestions

1 *Events* (intermediate)
Which of the following actions might happen in the events listed below? In each case, say how or why. It may not be possible to match them in every case.

Actions: To cry, to scream, to fight, to ride, to ring, to throw, to win, to hide, to draw, to burn, to shoot.

Events: A car crash, a party, a football match, a lesson.

As a follow-up activity students write a story in the past tense about one of the events above, using as many verbs as possible. (Many of these verbs are irregular.)

2 *Furniture and rooms* (beginners/elementary)
Which of the following pieces of furniture *could* be found in the different rooms?

Furniture: Bookshelf, cupboard, wardrobe, sofa, table, desk, record player, table lamp, basin.

Rooms: Kitchen, bedroom, living room, hall, dining room, study.

3 *Ways of reading* (upper-intermediate)

Ways of reading: To flick through something, to glance at something, to look something up, to read something carefully, to scan something, to read something aloud, to skim something.

Reading materials: A thriller, a newspaper (generally), a newspaper article, a dictionary, a book of photos, a history book, instructions for a new gadget you have just bought.

It would also be possible to devise similar exercises linking clothes and occasions, food and occasions, moods and types of books or films, ways of walking and events, etc.

Further reader activities

1 Devise a role play for further practice of vocabulary from the following:
   a) the text on page 120, 'Holidays go to the top of the perks list'.
   b) any suitable text you plan to use this week with your class.
2 Collect a set of pictures of disparate items you have taught your class recently. Use them as the basis for a narrative story similar to the one on page 150.
3 Experiment with one of the approaches described on page 150 which you have not used before. Either use the jogging picture story or a picture story of your own.

4 Devise a mime story to practise one of the following:
   a) something cooking
   b) a street event (e.g. an accident)
   c) 'make' versus 'do' (e.g. activities in the home).
5 Use one of the suggested topics for processes on page 156 and devise a set of items suitable for your class.

11 Games, questionnaires and problem solving

This last chapter of part C contains a 'mixed bag' of vocabulary practice activities. Most of these would be particularly useful for revision and further practice rather than presentation, and on the whole, they require very little preparation time. Many of the activities described would be useful as warmers or end-of-class activities.

i) PYRAMID GAME

Level: Intermediate upwards.
Suggested procedure: Choose about twelve lexical items you have taught in the previous few days and write them on a piece of paper in two columns. Thus:

Student A	Student B
a bend in the road	traffic lights
to skid	the boot of the car
the bumper	to swerve
to run someone over	to crash into something
foggy	a fork in the road
a zebra crossing	a careless driver

This vocabulary forms a clear lexical set but you may decide to make a more random selection.

Make as many copies of the columns as you need for your class and cut them in half. Put the students in pairs, facing each other, and give six of the items to one student in each pair. To this student explain that he has to define the words as quickly and clearly as possible so that student B can say what the word is. Student A can then go on to define the next word. He mustn't use any of the words on the card. It is usually clearer if you demonstrate to the group as a whole first:
e.g. Teacher: It's a long, yellow fruit with a skin you can't eat.
      Students: Banana.
When student A has defined all his words and student B has guessed them, give student B his group of words to define for student A.

It is useful at the end to discuss as a group how the students described their items; this can provide an ideal opportunity to introduce and develop different ways of paraphrasing and defining.

Comment: This activity is an enjoyable way of revising and, if done on a regular basis, can give students valuable practice in paraphrase, circumlocution, etc.

ii) COMMON FEATURES

Level: Advanced. (This game is a further practice activity for the material on page 140.)

Suggested procedure: On the blackboard draw two circles and add the vocabulary thus:

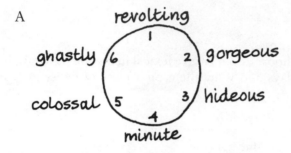

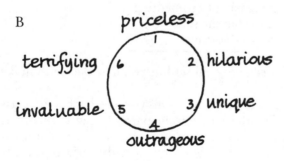

Divide the students into small groups and give each group a dice. All groups do the following activity at the same time.

One student in each group throws the dice twice; the first throw corresponds to dial A and the second to dial B. If, for example, he throws 5 the first time and 6 the second, his two words are 'colossal' and 'terrifying'. The group then has to make a note of the two words and think of something or someone which includes these two words in their meaning (e.g. King Kong). The next student in the group takes his turn to throw the dice and the groups thus build up a set of about five to six two-word combinations and an example for each.

Now bring the whole class together, and ask the first group to tell their *example* (i.e. King Kong). The rest of the class then have to decide which two adjectives from the circles were the ones they had thrown.

Comment: For a low level, the same activity could be done with simple vocabulary e.g.

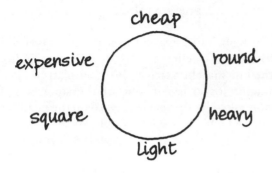

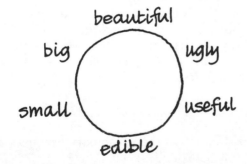

Note: Students may need more help from the teacher or a bilingual dictionary in finding examples if they are a lower level.

iii) NOUGHTS AND CROSSES

Level: All levels.

Suggested procedure: Draw two grids on the blackboard, filling in the squares on one grid with various headings and leaving the other one blank. The choice of headings depends entirely on the type of group and the items you wish to revise, here are two examples:

165

preposition	past tense	adjective		clothes	furniture	sport
opposite	noun	spelling		shopping	food	work
pronunciation	adverb	verb		transport	cinema, theatre, T.V.	health

Before the lesson you should have prepared three or four questions on each of your chosen headings.

Divide the class into two teams and explain that the object of the game is for each team to try and secure a straight line of noughts (or crosses) on the grid; the line may be vertical, horizontal, or diagonal. In order to get a nought (or cross) in one of the squares the team must answer a question asked by the teacher based on the heading of their selected square. So, if team A want a nought in the top left hand corner they must answer a question on prepositions e.g. complete the sentence 'I'm not very keen ... tennis'. If the team cannot answer the question they do not get their nought in the square, but the question is not passed to the other team. As the teams answer questions correctly you put the noughts and crosses onto the empty grid on the blackboard.

Comment: We first encountered this game (as applied to the EFL classroom) in the Teacher's Book to *Contact English 1* (Colin Granger and Tony Hicks, 1977). We have used it very successfully with a wide range of classes and found it to be a very enjoyable way of revising vocabulary items from previous lessons.

iv) PELMANISM

Level: Intermediate upwards (although the vocabulary examples given here would be upper-intermediate or advanced).

Suggested procedure: Write a list of partial synonyms which you wish to revise with your class (about eight to twelve pairs of words will be sufficient) e.g. man/guy, child/kid, a pound/a quid, mad/round the bend.

Write each of these items on small pieces of card:

a man	a guy	a child	a kid

duplicating your sets according to the size of your class.

Divide the students into groups of four to five and give them a set of cards which they place face down on a level surface in front of them. The first student turns up any two cards to see if they are partial synonyms; if they are, he keeps them, and if not, he turns them face down again, and the next player takes his turn. If the player turns up two partial synonyms (e.g. man/guy) he has to state the difference between them (i.e. 'guy' is more colloquial) to the satisfaction of his group. The winner is the student who accumulates most sets of cards. The game can be played several times in a row.

Comment: Although any vocabulary items can be recycled in this way, this is a particularly useful activity for revising items which students need to know for receptive purposes. With this particular example, the slang words may sound rather incongruous when spoken by students, but they may be useful items to recognise and understand in an English-speaking community.

v) QUESTIONNAIRE – 'MAKE' VERSUS 'DO'

Level: Intermediate.

Suggested procedure: Pre-teach the collocations of 'make' and 'do' listed in the questionnaire. You could display a set of visuals illustrating the vocabulary and ask the students to decide which verb ('do' or 'make') is used in each case; they could use dictionaries or shared knowledge to do this.

Practice: Give the students a copy of the questionnaire and ask them to carry out a class survey to find out whether these activities are predominantly carried out by men or women. Point out that they must use the appropriate verb in their question:

e.g. In your house, | who does the shopping?
| who makes the most money?

At the end of the group work, it may be fun to compile the results.

Comment: This is a controlled practice activity with a communicative aim. It also revises the 'household activity' vocabulary.

⟫→

'MAKE' AND 'DO' – a questionnaire

In your house, who *does* or *makes* things?
Ask the other people in your group and fill in the information about them.

Who *does* or *makes* these?

	a man	a woman	either	who? you / your brother / wife / friend / father / etc.
the shopping			X	Juan or mother or sister
the washing-up				
the cooking				
the bed(s)				
the cleaning				
the decorating				
the most money				
the ironing				
a mess				
most of the decisions				

© 1986 Cambridge University Press

168

vi) MARRIAGE QUIZ (*LASDE*)

Level: Upper-intermediate.

Suggested procedure: Allow students to work together to discover the meaning of the italicised words using shared knowledge and dictionaries. Ask them to guess the answers to any questions they don't know: this will make the correct answers more interesting! This activity can be done as a team game with points awarded for good answers. Students can then discuss the differences between marriage in Great Britain and in their own countries.

Comment: Another approach here would be to give the students extra supplementary reading material; *Life in Britain* (Brookes and Fraenkel, 1982) has a paragraph on weddings where the answers to some of the questions could be found. Alternatively, this information could be given to half the group who in the feedback could then correct the guesses of the other half. If is often possible to link vocabulary teaching and cultural information in this way.

STUDENT ACTIVITY

MARRIAGE QUIZ – **see how much you know about English marriage!**

1 When do people *get engaged*?
2 What happens to the *bride* and *groom* during a wedding?
3 Why wouldn't you see any women at a *stag party*?
4 What happens in a *registry office*?
5 Who pays for the *reception*?
6 If you were asked to *toast* the bride and groom, what would you say?
7 Where do most people spend their *honeymoon*?
8 Why can't *a bachelor* also be *a bigamist*?
9 Can anyone be *a spinster*?

© 1986 Cambridge University Press

vii) HAIR PROBLEM SOLVING ACTIVITY (MARRIAGE LINES)

Level: Upper-intermediate upwards.

Suggested procedure: This activity is a useful follow up to the semantic field exercise on page 104. Students can either do this in pairs in class or on their own for homework.

(The answers are: 1 Mr Foyle's   2 dark hair   3 Mr Foyle is bald.)

Comment: Try doing this activity yourself. It's virtually impossible to do it without repeatedly mumbling the relevant vocabulary either aloud or 'in your head'. It would be simple to vary the vocabulary and for example, describe the people as living in a cottage, detached house, semi-detached house, terraced house, etc.

STUDENT ACTIVITY

Marriage Lines**

Messrs Lagan, Foyle, Bann and Erne are neighbours. Three of them are married. One of the four is bald, one redheaded and one dark-haired.

Mr Erne isn't redheaded, nor is he dark-haired, but is married.
Mr Lagan isn't bald nor is he fairhaired, but is single.
Mrs Bann is blonde but her husband is neither dark-haired nor bald.
Mr Foyle doesn't have either fair or dark hair.
Mr Erne's wife is dark-haired while the bald-headed man has a redheaded wife.
  With this set of facts, can you work out the following:

1. Whose wife is a redhead?
2. What colour hair has the single man?
3. Mrs Foyle's husband has which hair colour?

(from *Gyles Brandreth's Book of Puzzles and Brainteasers.*)

Further reader activities

1 Devise a quiz (similar to the one on p. 169) which practises/revises vocabulary on one of the following topics:
  a) politics   d) entertainments
  b) education   e) sports
  c) illnesses
2 Devise a pelmanism game (see p. 166) with twenty paired words to revise one of the following:
  a) work vocabulary (see p. 136 for some examples)
  b) 'extreme' adjectives (see p. 141)
  c) clothes vocabulary (e.g. 'jeans' versus 'trousers', 'boots' versus 'shoes', 'shirt' versus 'blouse')
3 Devise a questionnaire to practise/revise relevant vocabulary for one of the following:
  a) You and your personality.
  b) Holidays and travel.
  c) Leisure activities.

12   Vocabulary in course books

In many teaching situations, teachers have little or no control over the choice of course books or materials prescribed for their students; this is often the choice of governments, Education Committees or Directors of Studies. Inevitably some teachers will be satisfied with the course book they are using while others will find it a hindrance. This final chapter is concerned with course books and how they can be used and adapted with regard to the teaching of lexis.

Although historically the importance of vocabulary has been minimised, some of the more recently published EFL course books have adopted a systematic approach to vocabulary learning and have become increasingly aware of the importance of developing vocabulary learning strategies. One distinct advantage that course book writers and materials designers have over practising classroom teachers is that they have easy access to word frequency counts and other checklists and the time to ensure that high priority items are introduced at appropriate stages of the syllabus and recycled where possible. Clearly this reduces the work-load on teachers tremendously provided, of course, that the selection and integration is appropriate and effective.

Inevitably there will be occasions when teachers do not agree with the selection and organisation of lexis in their course book. To enable you to assess the vocabulary component of your course book systematically, we have included the following checklist, which should help you to determine the amount of work which has been done for you and how much you will need to adapt and supplement the lexical items and materials.

12.1   Checklist

I   SELECTION

Is there a lexical syllabus?
Begin by looking at the introduction to the teachers' book to see whether it has a section on vocabulary; this section should mention how vocabulary items have been selected (based on word frequency counts, subjective

selection or simply as a vehicle for structural or notional/functional practice). Examine the list of items selected for a few units to see whether they are useful and relevant to your students; you may need to pay particular attention here to the cultural appropriacy of items. Notice whether the students' book or the teachers' book contains an index of new lexical items either at the end of each unit or at the back of the book.

How are vocabulary items grouped?

Look back at chapter 4 to remind yourself of the ways in which vocabulary can be grouped to facilitate learning. Does your course book make use of any groupings of this type, or are all items taught purely on an *ad hoc* basis?

How many items are introduced at once?

Bearing in mind your teaching situation, is the amount of 'productive' vocabulary to be acquired (per lesson or per hour) insufficient, sufficient or excessive for your learners?

2 LINGUISTIC CONSIDERATIONS

To what extent does the course book assist both learner and teacher in clarifying meaning, dealing with style and connotation, or contrasting items which cause difficulty? Does it provide phonemic transcriptions and indicate the part of speech of new items? How thoroughly does it deal with the use of items? (This will radically affect the amount of preparation and teacher intervention required, and the extent to which the course may be used as self-access material.)

3 METHODOLOGY

What learning approaches are selected?

Does the course book aim both to develop vocabulary learning strategies and provide learners with a useful selection of items for productive use? Notice whether there is systematic attention to contextual guesswork and dictionary training, or whether the systems of vocabulary such as word building are sufficiently covered.

Does the teachers' book suggest teaching procedures?

Some teachers' books provide useful guidelines on presenting and clarifying the meaning of lexical items or groups of items.

Are practice and testing activities provided?

Check to see whether the book contains a variety of practice activities, and if the vocabulary is used in realistic communication wherever possible. Where testing occurs, are students required simply to recognise the meaning of the items or to use them? (Practice and testing are common areas where teachers need to supplement many course books, so it is worth looking at this very closely.)

Is the vocabulary recycled?

Notice whether new language items are recycled through different skills activities and whether they occur in a variety of contexts. It is unreasonable to expect that every new language item should be consistently recycled throughout a course book, but one can expect that in consolidation units key items should be revised, and in a set of course books that topic areas and lexical sets are progressively revised and expanded.

How are learners encouraged to consolidate and widen their vocabulary outside the classroom?

Look carefully at suggested homework activities and workbooks. Some provide exercises to consolidate vocabulary presented in the course book, and/or provide scope for self-access work. This is particularly important where no 'street learning' is taking place.

Does the course book contain useful visual material?

Visuals can be used to illustrate meaning; check whether the visuals selected do this effectively.

Does the course book anticipate vocabulary needed for skills activities?

Begin by looking at listening and reading materials, and notice whether the teachers' book or the students' book anticipate difficulties with key vocabulary items. Similarly, for speaking and writing activities, see if essential productive vocabulary is suggested. If not, it may be necessary to 'rehearse' the activity (perhaps with teaching colleagues) to identify which items would be useful to pre-teach.

12.2 Extracts from course books

We have chosen to look at extracts from three popular and widely-used course books; each one illustrates different problems facing the teacher with regard to vocabulary teaching. The amount of preparation required by the teacher varies from example to example. In extracts 2 and 3 particularly, where more teacher intervention is called for, we have provided sample activities to supplement the published material.

EXTRACT FROM *STUDYING STRATEGIES*

The materials and activities in the unit before the extract include a text about Sri Lanka (which contains some of the vocabulary in ex. 2), some structural work on present and past participles and passives, and a noun/verb stress exercise (e.g. 'import/im'port). We have chosen to include this extract because we think it is a good example of integrated vocabulary work. Firstly, the items are recycled in all four skills through meaningful and relevant practice activities. Secondly, it is conveniently grouped by theme which is not only helpful for testing and practice but also for storage. Consequently it is apparent to the learner which items he is learning. Finally, we think that most of the lexis included will be relevant to the majority of learners.

This material is clearly very exploitable. There are, however, certain pitfalls for learners, and teachers will need to intervene to clarify certain points and/or to direct learners to their dictionaries. One difficulty arises in the testing activity in exercise 2: the difference between 'area or landscape' and 'type of land' is difficult to define. ('Volcanic' could refer to the contours or the soil type, so the category is rather ambiguous. Similarly, on *SS* page 95, 'jungle' is categorised under 'main vegetation' whereas on page 96, it is an area.) It may be advisable to ask students to leave these two categories to the end, or simply tell them to put the adjectives (i.e. hilly, flat, rural, arable, rocky, fertile) under 'type of land'. This then highlights another difficulty: if students are to use these items accurately, they will need to identify the parts of speech and make a

1. Study the list of words below and classify them under the following headings, like this:

> *Area or landscape:* desert
> *Climate:* cold
> *Type of land:* volcanic
> *Natural resources (non-edible):* gold
> *Natural resources (edible):* sugar, crops
> *Natural disasters:* flood

There are six words for each group.

famine	coal	coffee	iron ore
temperate	humid	avalanche	fertile
flat	plain	rocky	tea
hilly	jungle	rubber	mountains
valley	earthquake	arable	dry
rural	lake	tropical	drought
maize	rice	timber	wet
potatoes	hurricane	Mediterranean	oil
forest fire	minerals	fruit	forest

note of derivatives (e.g. volcano/volcanic, mountain/mountainous, a flood / to flood, etc.). Dictionary work is one possible solution here, and it also allows students to check the pronunciation of certain difficult items (e.g. famine, drought, fertile, hurricane, all of which may be subject to difficulty through mother-tongue interference). Finally, it will be necessary to highlight difficulties of collocation e.g. to suffer from drought, famine, etc.

Unit 12

2. Suggest the name of a place which:

– grows coffee
– suffers from famine
– produces oil
– has forests and lakes
– has jungle vegetation

– suffers from drought
– has a temperate climate
– is mountainous
– has arable farmland
– produces iron ore

3. Writing

Notice how some of these words are used in the following paragraph about Britain:

Britain is said to have a *temperate* climate. In the south and parts of the midlands, the land is very *arable* and many different sorts of *crops* are grown. The north can be quite *hilly* and in parts of Scotland and Wales you can find *mountains* and *lakes*. As regards natural resources, Britain produces *coal* in the midlands and in Wales, and has its own *oil* source in the North Sea. Apart from *floods* and the occasional *drought*, Britain is fortunate to escape many of the serious disasters that hit other countries.

Look at the photograph of Bora Bora and the information in the chart. Write a paragraph about Bora Bora similar to the one above, using the information given.

BORA BORA

Climate: tropical
Land: fertile: palmtrees, prickly pears
Natural resources: coconuts, fish, sun and water: ideal for tourism
Danger from natural disasters: hurricanes, tornadoes

Either write a similar paragraph about your own country
or write a longer composition, using the text on Sri Lanka as a guide.

4. Discuss and then write your reasons for preferring to live in one or other of the following:

Switzerland or Sri Lanka
Southern California or Australia
Britain or the USA

Use this guide:

Although ....., I would prefer to live in ..... There are several reasons why. *In the first place,* (mention the climate). *Secondly,* (mention the type of landscape, natural features, etc.). *Thirdly,* (mention way of life/the question of natural disasters and anything else you think is relevant).

❸ 🔊 Listening

Listen to a Senegalese student describing the region where he lives in Africa. Make notes under the topic headings in Number 2, Exercise 1. Write a short paragraph describing the region.

❹ Writing

You have been shipwrecked in the South Pacific. You managed to float on a raft with a few of your possessions to a deserted island ...

Describe your first impressions of the island and how you spent your first day: how did you get food and drink, where did you sleep, etc? Start your composition like this:

'I looked around me in wonder. Was I really on a desert island? .....'

End it like this:
'And so I lay down to sleep, exhausted after the long day and wondering what the next day would bring.'

175

EXTRACT FROM *STREAMLINE CONNECTIONS*

23 Four disasters

Good evening. Our programme tonight is about disasters. This year there have been fires, plane crashes, earthquakes, and volcanic eruptions. All our guests tonight have survived disasters.

Hi! I'm Bill Daniels. I live in Chicago. I was working in my office on the 28th floor of a skyscraper. I was dictating some letters to my secretary when the fire-bell rang. I rushed out to the lift but it wasn't working. The stairs were full of thick smoke. We couldn't go down, so we had to go up to the roof. When we got there some people were waiting calmly. Others were shouting and screaming wildly. A helicopter managed to land on the roof and rescued six of us before the building collapsed.

My name's Martha Huggins. I was on holiday in the South Pacific and I was staying on Pogohiti, a small island. I was having a rest when the volcano erupted. The noise woke me up. I looked through the window. Everybody was running towards the harbour. I just put on a coat, and ran to the harbour too. I managed to get on a ship. It was leaving when the lava hit the town.

Hello, I'm George Green. I'm a farmer. I was working in the field behind my house when I saw the plane. It was on fire. Smoke was coming from the engines, and it was coming down fast. I was running towards my house when it crashed into the trees behind me. I heard a terrible explosion . . . when I woke up, I was lying in a hospital bed.

Good evening. My name's Michael Purt. My wife and I were staying with friends on Santa Monica in the Caribbean. We were having dinner when the earthquake began. Everything shook. All the plates and food fell onto the floor. We were picking everything up when the ceiling fell onto us. We couldn't move, and we had to wait for three hours before help arrived.

As the unit is designed to revise and consolidate previously taught structures rather than introduce any new ones, this would seem to be the ideal opportunity to complement the grammar revision with the presentation and practice of new lexis. The teachers' book makes reference to the vocabulary in the unit in the following way:

Key Vocabulary

ceiling	*hospital*	*go down*
coat	*island*	*manage to (do it)*
damage	*lava*	*move*
disaster	*lift*	*pick up*
earthquake	*plate*	*rescue*
engine	*programme*	*rush*
explosion	*rest*	*scream*
farmer	*roof*	*shake*
field	*skyscraper*	*survive*
fire	*smoke*	*thick*
fire-bell	*volcano*	*usual*
floor	*cause*	*calmly*
food	*collapse*	*towards*
harbour	*dictate*	*on fire*
helicopter	*erupt*	*full of*
help		

We feel that this type of list is not very helpful for the teacher. By including so many items from the texts, the authors give no indication of what is really essential to an understanding of the texts, or what they consider to be the most useful items for the students to learn. Sensibly, the authors have integrated a number of items (over half of the list) previously presented in this book or the earlier *Streamline Departures*, although this distinction between vocabulary intended for revision and vocabulary that will be new, is not made apparent. And finally, they have omitted any information about the grammar, phonology or potential conceptual difficulty of the new items. A teacher rigorously following the procedural instructions (which do not mention how and when important lexical items should be taught) will find himself asking the students comprehensive questions on the text that include lexical items which have not been taught e.g. text 4: 'What were they doing when the *ceiling* fell onto them?' As the students by this time will have heard and repeated the line: 'We were picking everything up when the ceiling fell onto us', it is possible that some students will have retained the items in their short term memory and so be capable of answering the question. This does not, however, indicate that the students have any clear understanding of either 'ceiling' or 'pick up'.

We have not singled out this particular book for criticism because it is unique, but because we believe it to be fairly representative of many

Vocabulary in course books

English language course books and reflects the neglect of vocabulary teaching in recent years. This book, along with many others, charts a very clear structural path with detailed teaching notes for presentation and practice. Unfortunately, vocabulary does not receive the same attention and so teachers may find that this is the area where they will need to supplement the course book most carefully.

The following suggestions indicate a few ways in which the vocabulary contained in the above unit could be tackled more thoroughly. *Obviously, we are not suggesting that all these activities should be used with one class!*

Suggestions

PRE-READING OR PRE-LISTENING ACTIVITIES

You will need to consider first of all which items the students will need in order to grasp the gist of the news stories, and decide which of these would be useful as part of the students' productive vocabulary. Our suggestions are as follows: a disaster, a skyscraper, to be on fire, a volcano (to erupt), to crash into something/ a plane crash, an earthquake.

One approach would be to ask the students to cover the texts and look at the pictures. Explain that the pictures represent four disasters which people have lived through. Ask them to discuss in pairs/groups which key vocabulary items are important to each picture. (If you restrict them to two items per picture, you should avoid a vocabulary 'swamp'.) It is quite possible that some of the key items will be unknown; monolingual classes may wish to ask their teacher for a translation of the target item or use the picture to ask, 'How do you say this in English?' The vocabulary can then be highlighted and practised in a relatively controlled way. (Incidentally, the last picture is rather ambiguous and will need clarifying.)

A further pre-reading or pre-listening activity would be to ask the students to predict in which news story certain vocabulary items might occur, or to take out certain sentences from the stories and ask the students (through shared knowledge and the use of dictionaries) to decide which picture they refer to:

e.g. ...I rushed out to the lift but it wasn't working...
...it was leaving when the lava hit the town...
...smoke was coming from the engines...
...the ceiling fell on us...

1 *Deducing meaning*

Certain items in these news stories can be deduced because of syntactic or general knowledge clues:

e.g. roof, '... we couldn't go down, so we had to go up on the *roof.*'

Having shown students how to deduce one or two items, it should be possible for them to deduce others e.g. to land, to collapse, to erupt, to shake, harbour, ceiling.

2 *Cause and effect*

This activity not only tests gist understanding but requires the students to use certain items of vocabulary productively.

STUDENT ACTIVITY

Complete the sentences the same way as in the example, using the vocabulary in the list below:

    to be on fire   a fire   smoke   earthquake   to crash

e.g. The building was full of smoke because ....

    (The building was full of smoke because it was on fire.)

1 The people went on the roof because ....
2 The building collapsed because ....
3 The plane exploded because ....
4 The farmer ran to his house because ....
5 The plates fell on the floor because ....
6 The plane crashed because ....

3   General knowledge quiz
e.g. 1 What type of building is the Empire State Building?
      2 What is Etna?
      3 What happened at Mount St Helens?
      4 What disaster is common in both Japan and Southern Italy?
      5 What happened in Brighton in October 1984?

Other questions can be devised which will elicit the target vocabulary in a similar way, and can be written in accordance with the cultural knowledge of the class.

4   Word building
This is a simple transformation exercise:
e.g. There was *an explosion.*
      The plane........................ .
      (The plane *exploded.*)
1 The *plane crashed.* There was........................ .
2 The skyscraper *was on fire.* There was........................ .
3 The helicopter *rescued* the people on the roof. There was a dramatic
   ....
4 They waited three hours before *help* arrived. Someone........................them.
5 The *eruption* of the volcano was sudden. The volcano suddenly
   ....

5   Pronunciation
Ask the students to fill in the following grid using the past tenses of the verbs in the list.

to erupt   to manage   to explode   to wait   to scream   to collapse   to look   to rescue   to crash

/d/	/t/	ɪd/
		erupted
		.

(You may decide to highlight the phonological rule for regular past tenses i.e. voiced sounds are followed by the voiced /d/, unvoiced sounds are followed by the unvoiced /t/ and verbs ending in 'd' and 't' are followed by /ɪd/.)

Students can then be asked to make up sentences using the verbs to practise the pronunciation point.

6   Discussion

Begin by clarifying the meaning and form of the items on the left-hand side of the table below.

	Fire in a skyscraper	*Plane crash*	*Earthquake*	*Volcano*
frightening				
difficult to escape				
difficult to control				
common				
long-lasting				

Having organised the students into pairs or groups, ask them to rate each disaster in terms of the criteria given on the left. This will provide them with scope for creativity and meaningful practice of the target items.

7   Creative writing

Divide your class into pairs or small groups and give each a piece of paper with a set of four to six vocabulary items. These can be items from the news stories and items from previous lessons which will give an opportunity for revision:

e.g. 1.

> to scream
> the suburbs
> to be on fire
> ceiling
> roof
> to rescue

2.

> to manage to do something
> to crash into something
> smoke
> to land
> to breathe
> a disaster

Ask each pair or group to incorporate the vocabulary into a brief news-flash. Explain that each pair/group will then read out their newsflash and the rest of the class will then have to spot which items they were asked to incorporate. (Cunning groups will work hard to use many items from the lesson to make the listed items seem less obvious.)

EXTRACT FROM *MEANINGS INTO WORDS INTERMEDIATE*

So far we have looked at course book examples which require additional activities or guidance to help with the teaching of vocabulary contained in the respective units. Quite often, though, students find their greatest need is for vocabulary that is not directly encountered in the course book but arises as a consequence of the suggested practice activities. For the teacher this poses the problem of anticipating where this need will arise and also anticipating precisely what items should be taught to satisfy these needs.

Consider the following extract from *Meanings into Words Intermediate*:

12.3 HEADLINE NEWS

Practice

Look at the newspaper headlines below, and explain what they mean.

Example

> **Express derailed at 90 mph**

An express train was derailed while it was travelling at 90 miles per hour.

Boeing 747 hijacked over Atlantic
150 arrested in anti-nuclear demonstration
Ambassador's son kidnapped on way to school
Tomatoes thrown at Minister during speech
Man with bomb arrested at Heathrow
GOLFER STRUCK BY LIGHTNING

Writing

Choose one of the headlines and develop it into a paragraph. Add any details you like, and add at least one more event.

Example An express train was travelling at 90 m.p.h. on the main line from London to Manchester last night when it was derailed by a tree which was lying on the line. Fortunately, no-one was killed, although 30 passengers were taken to hospital suffering from minor injuries.

This activity is designed to provide further practice of the past simple and past continuous, and the use of 'when' and 'while' to link past events and the circumstances in which they took place. This is presented in the unit prior to the activity above.

The six headlines may present certain lexical difficulties e.g. hijacked/kidnapped/struck by lightning, but it is the extended writing activity that is likely to pose the greatest problems as students try to elaborate on the headline stories. If the lexical difficulties become too acute the intended structural practice is in danger of being either forgotten or neglected, and the activity may not fulfil its original purpose. To prevent this from happening we can try to anticipate the essential items and teach them prior to the structural presentation or perhaps in a preceding lesson. Four of the headlines i.e. the hijacking, the kidnapping, the demonstration, and the airport arrest, are all quite closely linked so it may be advisable to concentrate on the lexis relevant to these events, and ignore the remaining two headline stories.

To begin with, write the four events on the blackboard in four separate columns:

a hijacking	a kidnapping	a violent demonstration	a man arrested at an airport with a bomb

Any unknown items can be explained at this point with the addition of the relevant derivatives i.e. hijacker / to hijack, kidnapper / to kidnap, demonstrator / to demonstrate. Then write the following list of words on the board below the four columns:

to threaten	somebody to do something	a weapon
ransom		a hostage
blow up		to assassinate
to protest (against something)		to land
to hide		to release
to take part in something		

The students must decide which words are likely to occur in the context of the four events, and put the words in the appropriate column: you should explain that some of the items may be relevant to more than one event. This activity will require dictionaries and is best done in pairs or groups so that the students can share their knowledge and discuss the meaning of the different items. You will have to monitor this activity carefully and help with explanations or clarification where necessary; this may be with individual pairs/groups, or in some cases the whole class.

When you are satisfied that the students have a reasonable grasp of the new items, each pair/group can be assigned a particular event and told to use the new words in example sentences related to their event. Afterwards the students can look at all the different sentences compiled while you check that the items have been used correctly. The students should now be in a position to undertake the writing activity in the course book, without too much fear that lexical needs will distract them from the task of employing the target structures accurately and effectively. At the same time, of course, the activity will be providing useful consolidation of previously presented vocabulary.

Key ⚷

Chapter 1

Activity 1, page 3

You may be forgiven for getting some of the answers wrong; they are all common examples of mother-tongue interference, in these cases leading to communicative error. The importance of this type of error is that it may not be immediately apparent to the listener and can therefore cause considerable misunderstanding.

1 A free education. The student translated *scuola pubblica* (which means State school) directly into English.
2 Factual information. In this case the student chose 'great' rather than 'big', not realising that 'great' here would mean 'marvellous'.
3 Take a train. A Mexican student would probably be more used to American English where 'subway' is the equivalent of 'underground train'.
4 Poverty-stricken. *Suburbios* is the shanty area outside a city.
5 His diary. *Agenda* in French means a diary, whereas in English it is a list of the proposed subjects for discussion at a meeting.
6 No. *Station de ski* might more accurately be translated as ski resort. This is clearly interference of French rather than Arabic for this Tunisian speaker.

Activity 2, page 3

French	German	Spanish
terrible = great, fantastic	*aktuell* – modern,	*contenta* = happy,
librairie = bookshop	up-to-date	content
furieux = furious	*singen* = to sing	*embarazada* = pregnant
préparer = to prepare	*famos* = great, fantastic	*tímido* = timid, shy
canne à pêche = fishing	*Menü* = set meal	*constipado* = having a
rod	*kommen* – to come	cold
		movimiento =
		movement

Clearly, some of the items above are easily guessable and are true friends, but others are not. These are known as 'false cognates' or 'false friends'.

Activity 3, page 4

No key.

Key

Activity 4, page 5

1 to jump the queue	6 to take someone/something for granted
2 to give someone a lift	7 to make the most of | the time
3 to fall asleep	it
4 inside out	8 off the beaten track
5 a write-off	

Activity 5, page 6

All the errors indicate that the student has encountered the word in at least one of its grammatical values, and is either using that form in place of the correct form, or is attempting to guess the correct form from previous knowledge e.g. 'to devaluate' is a logical guess from 'devaluation', as it is possible to make transformations like this in many other cases. Such errors indicate the importance of highlighting derivatives. In some cases, the students can be given some help in word formation (see p. 47). In other cases, where the rules are not so generative, the teacher will need to teach the individual examples (as in 'to complain'/ 'to make a complaint').

Activity 6, page 6

The student seems to need particular help with verb patterns; in other words, how to use verbs to form grammatically correct sentences (e.g. to advise + object + infinitive).

Activity 7, page 7

Group 1: All have irregular past tense and past participle.
Group 2: All are normally followed by a particular preposition.
Group 3: Stative versus dynamic verbs. These verbs are not used in progressive tenses in their most common meanings.
Group 4: Are usually followed by a gerund construction.

Activity 8, page 7

1 Irregular plurals e.g. man, woman, wife, child, policeman (this latter example being similar in pronunciation in singular and plural).
2 Uncountable nouns e.g. luggage, information, advice, patience. Students often have difficulty with these as some of these items can be made plural in their own language.
3 No agreement of adjectives (so not heavys luggage).
4 Saxon Genitive problem e.g. women's.
5 Possessive adjectives and object pronouns e.g. their, her.
6 Articles.

Activity 9, page 7

Clearly, context determines the meaning of an item of vocabulary. The opposite of 'dry' in a very general sense may commonly be 'wet' e.g. a wet/dry day, but when collocated with particular nouns, the meaning changes; 'dry wine' being a contrast to 'sweet wine'. Obviously in language teaching this practice is common and often helpful (e.g. an obvious way to clarify the meaning of 'ugly' (person) is to contrast it with 'beautiful'). However, it is a technique which requires careful handling. When two items frequently 'co-occur' in this way (e.g. dry wine) they are said to form a *collocation*. (See p. 37.)

Activity 10, page 8

The following should have been crossed out.
1 He made a photo.   4 He did an investment
2 He got off the taxi.   5 The lesson broke out.
3 He lost the bus.

These are all examples of incorrect *collocations* (see previous exercise). They are frequently the result of mother-tongue interference but they may also be the result of superficial understanding of an item e.g. in the example 'the lesson broke out', it seems that the learner has understood 'to break out' simply to mean 'to begin'.

Activity 11, page 8

1 This approach, starting from the root verb, is often adopted in published materials. However, we can see little justification for this approach as the addition of the adverbial particle changes the meaning of the verbs and creates three multi-word verbs which are totally unrelated in meaning. It is also unlikely to be very memorable for the students.
2 The same applies to this approach. The vertical movement associated with the prepositional use of 'up' is seldom applicable when 'up' becomes an adverbial particle. If the adverbial particle does perform a more consistent function with regard to its effect on the meaning of the root verb e.g. 'up' adding a sense of completion to verbs such as 'drink up', 'do up', etc. (see pp. 34–5), then the approach is clearly more valid.
3 This approach is logical in that there is a contextual link between the different verbs which often allows the teacher better opportunities for further practice and possibly makes the verbs more memorable for the students. The danger of seeking out lexical sets is that it sometimes results in the inclusion of verbs which are either of little practical use or are inappropriate to the level of the students.
4 Considering the different meanings of one particular multi-word verb guards against the danger of assuming that a word will always have the same meaning. It is unusual, however, for the different meanings to be equally useful to the students. Such an approach is perhaps best suited for revision purposes with more advanced students.

Key

Activity 12, page 9

There are, of course, many possible answers here. Those we have listed are just some of the mistakes more frequently encountered in the classroom.

1 row–line   4 common–usual, typical
2 break–interval   5 some/any room–a place, a space
3 achieve–reach   6 seats–places, chairs; aisle–corridor

Students will often make this kind of mistake because of the semantic similarities between the different words, and it illustrates the enormous problem of usage accompanying vocabulary teaching.

Activity 13, page 9

Using their previous knowledge of English, students might make a reasonable attempt to pronounce 'vicarage', 'deniable', 'phrenology', 'wrestle', 'rectory' and 'knave'. These words, although difficult, at least conform to certain general principles of English pronunciation that students might be familiar with:

e.g. a) The /ɪdʒ/ pronunciation of '+age' at the end of 'vicarage'.
      b) The /trɪ/ pronunciation at the end of 'rectory'.
      c) The main stress on 'deniable' (o**O**oo), plus the /aɪ/ for 'i' and the /əbl/ for '+able' might be guessed from knowledge of 'reliable'.
      d) Students may not produce the correct weak forms in 'phrenology' /frəˈnɒlədʒɪ/ but their knowledge of other sciences e.g. biology, psychology, should enable them to place the stress correctly and thus provide a perfectly adequate pronunciation of the word.
      e) The silent letters in '*w*restle' and '*k*nave' are fairly logical for students at higher levels (as in '*w*rite', '*k*nife' and 'lis*t*en').

There are precedents for students correctly providing 'dough' /dəʊ/ and 'bough' /baʊ/ from their knowledge of 'though' and 'plough'. However, as '+ough' may be pronounced in seven different ways in English, and as there are no pronunciation rules applicable, these words are likely to be very difficult.

Nothing but a lucky guess is likely to produce the correct pronunciation of 'sew' /səʊ/, 'thyme' /taɪm/ and 'tomb' /tuːm/, as previous knowledge of the language would probably suggest /suː/, /θaɪm/ and /tɒmb/. The pronunciation of 'awry' /əˈraɪ/ would raise a few eyebrows and probably remain a complete mystery to the students.

These examples illustrate the fact that students can and should apply general principles of pronunciation when they meet new words, but it also shows the value of phonemics in solving some of the problems that students will certainly meet.

Activity 14, page 9

Each of the examples includes language that is, in some sense, inappropriate to the situation. The extent of this varies from example to example, and there may not be complete agreement on the changes that ought to be made, or even whether changes are necessary in every case. Here are some suggested amendments.

1 Hardly a serious blunder, but substituting 'won't be home', 'be home' and 'about' for the rather awkward 'will be absent', 'arrive home', and 'approximately', would give the passage the natural informal style it lacks.
2 'Land the company in a lot of trouble' is too colloquial beside the formal style used in the rest of the memo.
3 The awkward use of 'disturb' and 'endure' indicates that the speaker is either unfamiliar with the more colloquial 'bother' and 'put up with', or else is unaware that the situation calls for more informal language.
4 The use of 'my dear' is clearly wrong and could cause offence.
5 'Great strides', 'fantastically well', 'keep up' and 'terrific' appear rather chatty in the context of a formal piece of writing.
6 In this case, a native speaker would be more likely to express the idea by saying, 'I'm going to the pub with a friend'. The student's response shows that his understanding of 'meeting' and 'colleague' is inaccurate and the effect is a very stilted and over-formal response.

Activity 15, page 10

a) One word 'mass' is added in the second passage and other words are substituted:

Passage 1	Passage 2
solve my problems	end my nightmare
memory	nightmare
hit	smashed
...Sutcliffe with a hammer	the hammer-wielding killer
severity	savagery
serious	horrific

b) The effect of these substitutions is to incite greater hatred and anger towards Sutcliffe, and illustrates the emotive force of language. Students, particularly at higher levels, should be made aware of this.

Activity 16, page 12

There are certain concepts in this advertisement which one could describe as being socio-culturally specific, in this case to a particular group within British society. The idea of writing *to* a diary ('Dear Diary...') may well be alien to many cultures, as well as the concept of being 'upper-crust' in classless societies. The humour is very 'British' and cultural references apart, many nationalities may fail to see anything humorous about this advert. Probably one of the most obvious stumbling blocks is the proper names (and their associations) and place names. The socio-cultural associations will be discussed more fully on page 19.

Chapter 2

Page 13

For this exercise there are many possible answers – we have included here the most common examples.

Suitcase/briefcase: there is a difference of size and possibly shape, and the function of these bags is not the same.

Brochure/pamphlet/booklet/leaflet/prospectus: brochures give information about services which are paid for, such as holidays.

Dustbin / waste paper basket or bin / litter bin: dustbins are generally heavier and bigger than the others, are for private domestic use, have lids (unlike litter bins) and are usually kept outside (unlike waste paper bins).

T-shirt/vest. T-shirts are worn either under other clothes (like a vest) or on their own; they are generally more decorative.

Advertisement/notice: notices tend to give information, sometimes of services; advertisements generally sell something, e.g. a job, a car, soap.

Page 14

Again, there are many possibilities, but these are our suggestions:
leg of a person/chair, table, bed etc./animal
mouth of a person/jug/river/animal/cave/tunnel
branch of a tree/family/railway line/river/shop, bank etc./knowledge
top of a mountain/tree/page/list/building/profession
tail of a coat/animal/comet/aeroplane

Page 16

target/goal   a) Our | target is a profit of £50,000 for the coming year.
                          | goal
                  b) Montcrieff scored a fabulous goal in the second half.

shallow/superficial a) His approach to his studies is rather | shallow.
                                                               | superficial.
                  b) The water's very shallow here – let's paddle.

fetch/bring   a) Could you | fetch me my glasses? They're on the table.
                               | bring
                  b) Come to our party but don't forget to bring a bottle!

rush/hurry   a) I'm going to be late – I'll have to | hurry.
                                                          | rush.
                  b) The hostages decided to try to rush the terrorist to make him drop his gun.

think/believe   a) I | think | he'll be here this evening.
                       | believe |
                  b) I don't believe in Father Christmas.

Page 21

1 Emoluments: formal (usually financial).
2 Cosine: mathematics (technical, trigonometry).
3 A shrink: colloquial, US, usually humorous.
4 Hence: formal (e.g. a mile hence), but can be neutral (e.g. I've got a job – hence the new suit.).
5 To fancy something: colloquial.
6 Loo: colloquial, GB.
7 Communicative competence: language teaching register.
8 Bonkers: slang, GB.
9 Bairn: Scottish and Northern English.

Page 23

1 Poll = survey. More or less synonymous here.
2 Harmful = damaging. More or less synonymous here.
3 Onus = responsibility. Synonymous here but 'onus' is a much lower frequency item.
4 Minors = children. There is a stylistic difference; minors is a legal term.
5 Nasty = unpleasant. More or less synonymous here.
6 Smutty = dirty. (Filthy is slightly more extreme and pejorative.)
7 Biased = prejudiced. Prejudiced has negative connotations.

Page 25

1 dead–alive
2 true–false
3 same–different
4 animate–inanimate
5 imperfect–perfect

Page 26

1 Mary is Tom's sister.
2 Margaret is David's aunt.
3 Nigel is shorter than John.
4 I'm John Walker's patient.
5 Tom bought a tractor from Bill.
6 That blue Toyota belongs to John.
7 The film came before the geography lesson.

Page 27

There are many possibilities here, but we have included the most common ones.
1 boiling / very hot / hot / quite hot / warm / lukewarm / tepid / cool / cold / freezing
2 adore, love / like very much / like / quite like / not mind / dislike / hate, loathe, can't stand
3 fascinating / interesting / quite, fairly interesting / rather boring / boring / very boring / stultifying
4 fabulous, marvellous / very good / good / quite good / OK, average / not very good / mediocre / bad / awful, dreadful

191

Page 28

1 liquid/solid/gas
2 hearts/diamonds/spades/clubs
3 red/orange/yellow/green/blue/indigo/violet
4 Mercury/Venus/Earth/Mars/Jupiter/Saturn/Uranus/Neptune/Pluto
5 earth/fire/water/air
6 breakfast/lunch/(tea)/dinner (supper) – it depends on the context

Page 30

These are only *suggested* answers; there are many other ways.
b) To pass an exam – to fail an exam: 'Michael failed the exam, but Dirk got over 50% so he ...?'
c) Knife, fork, spoon: 'What's missing from this group – fork, spoon ...?' or 'What do you use when you eat your dinner?'
d) To own – to belong, also to own – to rent: 'This flat belongs to John, so John ...?' or 'I rent this flat from Mr Braddock. Mr Braddock ...?'
e) To sell – to buy: 'When you buy something in a shop, the shop assistant ...?'
f) In front of – behind: 'The blackboard is behind the teacher. The teacher is ...?'
g) Wide road – narrow road: 'What's the opposite of a narrow road?'
h) To rent – to let (e.g. a flat): 'Mr Howard is a landlord. He let his flat to me. I ...?'
i) Army, Navy, Air Force: 'What's missing from this group of three? Navy, Air Force ...?'
j) Gasoline, petrol: 'What's the American word for petrol?' or 'What's the difference between gasoline and petrol?'
k) Cardiac arrest, heart attack: 'What's another way of saying ...?' 'What's the difference?'
l) Awful, terrible: 'What's another word for terrible?'

Page 36

This list is subjective, and relates to our own teaching situation. We would teach 'it's up to you' and 'to get the sack' productively, and possibly 'tip of my tongue' and 'sleep like a log'. 'Fed up' would be useful receptively.

Page 40

This again is very subjective. It depends very much on the type of student you teach: a business English student would probably find 'do the housework' less useful than 'do business', but the opposite may be true for a general student.
a) At elementary/lower-intermediate: to do homework/an exercise, cooking, housework, somebody a favour ('Could you do me a favour?').
b) At upper-intermediate: those above, plus to do business, your hair, well/badly, right/wrong.

192

c) Post Cambridge First Certificate: 'to do your duty', 'harm', 'good'. (We do not feel 'to do someone an injustice', 'the honour of', are very useful to any general purpose foreign student.)

Chapter 3

Page 47

1 Readeress: a female reader, cf. authoress, actress.
2 Lunocracy: government or rule by lunatics, cf. democracy.
3 A gaolee: a person who is put in gaol (i.e. a prisoner), cf. employee, payee. (This use of the suffix '+ee' denotes passive.)
4 A toolery: a place where tools are made, c.f. bakery, a refinery, or, a collection of tools, cf. armoury, machinery. (Without the article, this could also be interpreted as the act of tool-making, cf. cookery.)
5 Doglet: a little dog (diminutive), cf. piglet.
6 Woolette: imitation wool, cf. suedette, leatherette.

Page 47

pre-war
ultra-conservative, ultra-modern

'pre+' = before (before the war);
'ultra+' = extremely (extreme conservative);

ex-conservative, ex-revolutionary
subhuman

'ex+' = former (former revolutionary);
'sub+' = below, less than (less than human).

Chapter 4

Page 60

4 **devil**
  4 *n.* Satan, any evil spirit, a bad man
  7 *n.* term of pity: *queer devil; poor devil*
5 **diagram** *n.*
5 **dial**
  5 *v.* telephone: *I've dialled them three times*
  6 *n.* face of a measuring device: *the dial on a radio*
5 **diameter** *n.*
3 **diamond**
  3 *n.* precious stone
  5 *n.* shaped in parallelogram: *diamond-pattern quilt*
4 **diary** *n.*
4 **dictate** *v.* speak for recording: *dictate to a secretary*
5 **dictation** *n.* passage that is dictated, activity of dictating

2 **dictionary** *n.*
1 **die**
  1 *v.* decease
  5 *v.* become weak: *interest in it died*
  6 *v.* long: *dying for a drink*
4 **differ**
  4 *v.* be unlike: *they differ in their tastes*
  6 *v.* not agree: *I differ from you about that*
2 **difference**
  2 *n.* unlikeness: *there's a big difference in attitude*
  4 *n.* gap: *there's a difference of nearly a kilo*
2 **different**
  2 *adj.* unlike: *this pencil is different from mine*
  3 *adj.* other: *this is a different way we are taking*

2 sociable, to shake, seat, recently
3 a) Beginner / elementary students: toilet, bath, shower, soap, toothbrush, toothpaste, razor (omit safety and electric but show razor covers both) possibly mirror, comb.
 b) Beginner / elementary students abroad: bath, shower, toilet, toothbrush, toothpaste, soap.
 c) Intermediate students in an English-speaking country: those above plus washbasin, tap, plug, sponge or flannel, brush.
 d) Intermediate students abroad: washbasin, mirror, towel, razor, tap, plug, comb.
Possibly towel rack, cistern could be omitted.

Page 66

There is no key answer for the first part of this activity.
1 Adults planning a holiday. Productively: to hurt, plasters, to be sick, diarrhoea, and for women, period. Receptively: dosage, harmful. Not at all: a splint, to faint, to come to, a wound.
2 Schoolchildren. Productively: to hurt, to be sick. Receptively: a wound, harmful, to faint. Not at all: the rest.
3 Nurses. Productively: a splint, a wound, to hurt, to faint, period, plasters, to be sick, diarrhoea. Receptively: dosage, to come to, harmful.

Chapter 5

Page 76

1 Tools: if students know items such as 'hammer', 'screwdriver', then give examples of types of tools. If not, show pictures or objects and tell students they are all tools. Beware of getting sidetracked into teaching names of tools if this is not central to your aim.
2 A turkey: a picture. Illustrate through context if you haven't a picture; if turkeys are eaten at festival times, for example.
3 A cigarette lighter: the object itself or a picture, or mime.
4 To get rid of something: a situation could bring several uses together here; for instance, you are going to live abroad and you don't want to take all your possessions with you. What can you do? Give them away, sell them, throw them away – all of these involve getting rid of something.
5 Boring: illustrate through contrast with 'interesting' and mime. Perhaps outline a simple situation.
6 Plump: on a scale perhaps, or by contrast (thin – fat; skinny – plump; skinny being slightly pejorative, plump being a more pleasant way to describe someone).
7 To choose: a situation; for instance, offer a student three different day trips or three TV programmes and ask him to select one.
8 Shrewd: translation if possible, as this is very subtle. If not, describe the actions of a shrewd person.

9 Appalling: give a synonym e.g. terrible.
10 To call something off: definition and situation; for instance, a party which had to be cancelled.
11 Mortgage: definition and explanation.
Translation is obviously an option with all the examples above.

Bibliography

Reference Sources

Longman Active Study Dictionary of English, Longman, 1983.
Longman Dictionary of Contemporary English, Longman, 1978.
Hornby, A. S., *Oxford Advanced Learner's Dictionary of Current English* (revised and updated), Oxford University Press, 1980.
McArthur, Tom, *Longman Lexicon of Contemporary English*, Longman, 1981.

Close, R. A., *A Reference Grammar for Students of English*, Longman, 1975.
Crystal, David, *A First Dictionary of Linguistics and Phonetics*, Andre Deutsch, 1980.
Gimson, A. C. and Ramsaran, S. M., *An English Pronunciation Companion*, Oxford University Press, 1982.
Hindmarsh, Roland, *Cambridge English Lexicon*, Cambridge University Press, 1980.
Leech, Geoffrey and Svartvik, Jan, *A Communicative Grammar of English*, Longman, 1975.
Meara, P. M. (compiled and edited), *Specialised Bibliography 3: Vocabulary in a second language*, Centre for Information on Language Teaching and Research, 1983.
Swan, Michael, *Practical English Usage*, Oxford University Press, 1980.
Tench, Paul, *Pronunciation Skills*, Macmillan, 1981.
van Ek, Jan and Alexander, Louis, *Threshold Level English*, published for and on behalf of the Council of Europe by Pergamon Press, 1975.
West, Michael (ed.), *A General Service List of English Words*, Longman, 1953.

Background Reading

Bransford, John, *Human Cognition*, Wadsworth, Inc., 1979. (This book also contains a fuller description of the experiments conducted by Brown and McNeill, 1966, and Freedman and Loftus, 1971.)
Bright, John and McGregor, Gordon, *Teaching English as a Second Language*, Longman, 1970.
Brumfit, C. J. and Roberts, J. T., *An Introduction to Language and Language Teaching*, Batsford Academic and Educational Ltd, 1983.
Hulse, Stewart H., Egeth, Howard and Deese, James, *The Psychology of Learning*, McGraw-Hill, Inc., 1981.

Hurford, James and Heasley, Brendan, *Semantics: a coursebook*, Cambridge University Press, 1983.

Leech, G., *Semantics* (second edition), Penguin, 1981.

Lyons, John, *Semantics* vols. 1 and 2, Cambridge University Press, 1977.

Lyons, John, *Language, Meaning and Context*, Fontana, 1981.

McDonough, Steven H., *Psychology in Foreign Language Teaching*, George Allen & Unwin, 1981.

Matthei, Edward and Roeper, Thomas, *Understanding and Producing Speech*, Fontana Paperbacks, 1983. (This book also contains a fuller description of the account of organisation in the memory by Forster, 1976, 1979.)

Palmer, F. R., *Semantics* (second edition), Cambridge University Press, 1981.

Pickett, G. D., *The Foreign Language Learning Process*, British Council ETIC, 1978.

Russell, Peter, *The Brain Book*, Routledge & Kegan Paul, 1979.

Smith, Frank, *Reading*, Cambridge University Press, 1978.

Stevick, E., *Memory, Meaning and Method*, Newbury House, 1976.

Widdowson, H. G., *Language Purpose and Language Use*, Oxford University Press, 1983.

Wilkins, D. A., *Linguistics in Language Teaching*, Edward Arnold, 1972.

Articles

Alptekin, C. and Alptekin, M., 'The question of culture: EFL teaching in non-English speaking Countries', *ELT Journal*, 38:1, January, 1984.

Meara, Paul, 'Vocabulary Acquisition: A neglected aspect of Language Learning', *Language Teaching and Linguistics:* Abstracts 13, 4, 1980.

Richards, Jack C., 'The role of Vocabulary Teaching', *TESOL Quarterly* vol. 10, No. 1, March, 1976.

Teachers' handbooks on vocabulary and related subjects

Bolitho, Rod and Tomlinson, Brian, *Discover English*, George Allen & Unwin, 1980.

French Allen, Virginia, *Techniques in Teaching Vocabulary*, Oxford University Press, 1983.

Morgan, John and Rinvolucri, Mario, *Once Upon a Time*, Cambridge University Press, 1983.

Ur, Penny, *Discussions that Work*, Cambridge University Press, 1981.

Wallace, Michael, *Teaching Vocabulary*, Heinemann Educational Books Ltd, 1982.

Williams, Eddie, *Reading in the language classroom*, Macmillan, 1984.

Wright, Andrew, Betteridge, David and Buckby, Michael, *Games for Language Learning*, Cambridge University Press, 1979.

Bibliography

Published Materials

Abbs, Brian/Freebairn, Ingrid with Clegg, John/Whitney, Norman, *Studying Strategies*, Longman, 1982.

Brookes, H. F. and Fraenkel, C. E., *Life in Britain*, Heinemann, 1982.

Granger, Colin, with illustrations by John Plumb, *Play Games with English*, Books 1 and 2, Heinemann Educational Books Ltd, 1980/1981.

Granger, Colin and Hicks, Tony, *Contact English*, Heinemann, 1977.

Fletcher, Mark and Birt, David, *Storylines*, Longman, 1983.

Kerr, J. Y. K., *Picture Cue Cards for Oral Language Practice*, Evans, 1979.

McArthur, Tom, *Using English Prefixes and Suffixes*, Collins, 1972.

Rudska, B., Channell, J., Putseys, Y. and Ostyn, P., *The Words You Need*, Macmillan, 1981.

Swan, Michael and Walter, Catherine, *The Cambridge English Course 1*, Cambridge University Press, 1984.

Underhill, Adrian, *Use Your Dictionary*, Oxford University Press, 1980.

Watcyn Jones, P., *Pair Work A & B*, Penguin, 1981.

Watcyn Jones, P., *Test Your Vocabularly* (1–4), Penguin, 1979.

Index